# DAPHNE'S

For Carmela

First published in Great Britain by Simon & Schuster UK Ltd., 1999

A Viacom company

1 3 5 7 9 10 8 6 4 2

Simon & Schuster UK Ltd.

Africa House

64–78 Kingsway

London WC2B 6AH

A CIP catalogue record for this book is available from the British Library.

ISBN 0-684-86049-X

# DAPHNE'S

## MODERN ITALIAN FOOD

MOGENS THOLSTRUP,

CHRIS BENIANS & LEE PURCELL

PHOTOGRAPHED BY JEAN CAZALS

TEXT BY SHEILA KEATING

SIMON & SCHUSTER

A VIACOM COMPANY

# contents

• *all recipes serve four unless otherwise stated*

# introduction

MY INTEREST IN COOKING STARTED WHEN I WAS A CHILD IN DENMARK. My grandmother had a large summer house on the beach, where the whole family would spend the month of July. Her dinners were legendary, and with parents, uncles, aunts and countless cousins and friends, most nights we would be nearly thirty around the dinner table. My grandmother loved food and entertaining, and was known to be quite demanding. She employed only the best cooks she could find in the country or often from abroad. One of my favourite moments would be standing in the kitchen during the early evening, watching their skilled hands prepare dinner. On other holidays during the rest of the year, I would travel with my parents through Europe, where we would visit a great number of restaurants, from humble bistros to Michelin-starred establishments. Although very young, I was always encouraged by my parents to try exciting dishes on the menu and I had my first grenouilles aged five.

Naturally I also started cooking at a very early age. However, the person who has influenced me most in my understanding of the Italian kitchen is my mother-in-law, Carmela. She taught me that a wonderful meal begins at the butcher, the fishmonger and the greengrocer, and that if you can't find the right ingredients in the best condition, it is better to do something different. From shopping and cooking with Carmela, I learned about porcini, truffles and young Roman artichokes on the stem that are so tender they don't even need cooking but can simply be shaved raw into a salad with Parmesan and lemon juice and extra virgin olive oil drizzled over them. I watched her make the most wonderful light-green pesto from basil leaves not much bigger than a fingernail, grown on the hills facing the sea in her home town of Genoa. Great cooking is about knowledge and flair. It is about knowing what to buy, where and when, and how to use the ingredients so that eventually recipes become superfluous, for inspiration rather than instruction. Good food is about appreciating that when you get a chance to buy the best, you shouldn't mess too much with it, but keep it simple. That is what I believe, and that, I hope, is the essence of Daphne's.

**Mogens Tholstrup**

# basics

 EVERY KITCHEN RELIES ON CERTAIN KEY INGREDIENTS IN THE CUPBOARD OR FRIDGE. WITH GOOD-QUALITY OILS AND VINEGARS, ANCHOVIES, PINE NUTS, FARMHOUSE CHEESES AND HERBS TO HAND, YOU HAVE THE BASIS FOR THE KIND OF SIMPLE, BOLDLY FLAVOURED DISHES COOKED AT DAPHNE'S.

## oils

A good extra virgin olive oil is one of the most important ingredients in any kitchen. At Daphne's the favourite oil is a peppery estate-bottled Tuscan one and the kitchen is full of bottles of this same oil infused with chillies, garlic, basil (see basil, page 15), anchovies (see anchovies, page 13) and orange or lemon zest. These oils are used to build up flavours in a dish; a little orange oil might be drizzled over grilled fennel, for example. When the flavouring ingredient has been added, the olive oil is left in a bowl in a bain-marie (a pan of simmering water) for several hours, letting the warmth bring the flavours alive. Then it can be stored in sterilised bottles for use as required. For chilli oil, the chillies are sliced in half lengthways, seasoned and cooked gently in a little oil, which is then topped up with more oil and left to infuse in the bain-marie. Garlic is cooked in the same way, and never used raw for infusing, while strips of orange or lemon rind are left in a warm place (e.g. above your cooker when it is being used) for several hours to dry out, then cracked slightly to release the maximum flavour, and warmed in the oil in the bain-marie.

## salted capers

Capers are used in many dishes in a similar way to anchovies, to give depth and introduce a little acidity, to cut through oiliness, just as lemon juice or vinegar would, rather than for their intrinsic flavour. For example, they can be pounded into anchovy & olive salsa (see page 27) or deep-fried, so that they puff up, and used as a garnish. Remember to rinse the salt off before use.

# Parmesan
The restaurant probably uses a whole weald, around 35 kilos, of Parmesan cheese a week, shaved onto salads and over risottos and other dishes. Parmigiano reggiano, matured for at least 24 months, is the very best Parmesan (still made in most places by hand) and is a perfect example of how the finest Italian foods need no interference. One of the unwritten rules of Italian cooking is that Parmesan doesn't go with fish, but there are a few exceptions, such as the crab salad on page 114 which is made with tuiles of Parmesan crisp: little rounds of grated Parmesan spread over a baking tray and baked in a medium oven for a few minutes until they become crispy. The nuttiness of the Parmesan works beautifully with the flavour of the crab.

# truffle oil
White truffle oil from Alba is an essential luxury; glorious drizzled over porcini, pasta or grilled vegetables — especially courgettes — or over meat or fish. Truffle oil is essentially olive oil infused with the unique smell and flavour of truffles. The cheapest merely taste and smell like a scented oil, often quite artificial, but the best encapsulate the clean, earthy flavour of the truffle itself. Good truffle oil isn't cheap, but the idea is to appreciate and respect it and use it sparingly, so a small bottle goes a long way.

# balsamic vinegar
Darkly fruity, its sweetness tempered with acidity, balsamic vinegar has been produced in the ancient Italian city of Modena for centuries. During the surge in popularity of Italian ingredients in the early 1990s, it was often over-used and abused, but now that a sense of moderation has taken over it has found a well-deserved place in many store-cupboards. The vinegar, which is produced from the juice of cooked Trebbiano grapes and aged in a series of wooden barrels of different sizes and woods from juniper to oak, can be anything from a few years old to the precious 50-year-old. Some cheaper vinegars may be a blend of white wine vinegar and balsamic, so be prepared to pay a little extra and look for the label 'aceto balsamico tradizionale di Modena'. In the Daphne's kitchen younger vinegars are used to intensify flavours in sauces which are being reduced down, for example for serving with foie gras. Older vinegars are used for finishing dishes. A splash of balsamic can really lift the flavour of fish or scallops. Try pan-frying scallops briefly in very hot oil, then, when you take them out, add a little balsamic vinegar to the pan juices, allow to bubble for a minute or so, then pour over the scallops.

# pine nuts

Resinous pine nuts are a key ingredient in pesto and for adding a lovely nutty bite to virtually any salads. In Liguria they are even added to fish stews. They can be toasted first in a dry pan over a low heat for a few minutes, but to really bring out their richness and flavour, sauté them very gently in foaming unsalted butter, as you would do with almonds, turning them all the time, until they are golden on each side, then drain and season with a little salt.

# bouquet garni

Bouquet garni is a bag or bunch of vegetables and/or herbs which is used to infuse flavour into slowly cooked dishes, such as casseroles or pots of borlotti beans, and which is removed at the end of cooking time. A bouquet garni is essential for cooking pulses, whose starchiness cries out to absorb added flavour. It can be simply made from a piece of carrot, leek and celery tied together with string, along with a bay leaf (the classic bouquet garni herb), and other strong, hard herbs, such as rosemary, oregano and marjoram. The softer herbs, such as basil and parsley, will simply dissolve, so are always added to dishes at the last moment.

# anchovies

Pounded into anchovy & olive salsa (see page 27), melted into a rich oil, or incorporated in the dressing for a Caesar salad (see page 45), anchovies make a major contribution to the Daphne's style of cooking. Because they are used to add depth to a dish, rather than as a single identifiable ingredient, even people who say they hate anchovies find they love the flavour of dressings made with them. Anchovy oil is tossed through pasta to bring together ingredients like radicchio, walnuts, endive and chicory. It can be used to marinate vegetables before chargrilling, or for serving with a powerfully flavoured vegetable like chargrilled courgettes. It works well with robust fish like roast salmon but would overpower very delicate fish. Anchovy oil is made by cooking the anchovies very gently in plenty of olive oil with some shallots and garlic over a whole day, until the anchovies almost dissolve into the oil. The finished oil is stored in sterilised bottles. When buying anchovies look for the biggest, whole salted red-fleshed fish. Before using, rinse off the salt, pat the anchovies dry and carefully pull the fillets away from the bones.

# vegetable stock

A light neutral vegetable stock (see page 20) is a good ingredient to have on hand for use in pastas and risottos or for braising vegetables. It is there purely to provide background flavour, adding something a little more than just water, so it shouldn't be too strong, or taste overly of one vegetable. In a restaurant kitchen it is an easy thing to have on the go, because vegetable trimmings are always on hand; in the domestic kitchen it is probably easier to make up a batch and freeze it in ice-cube trays.

# salt & pepper

Seasoning is at the very heart of good cooking. When chefs overseason it is often because they are trying too hard, pushing the flavours as far as they can and then going a little too far. Fish should always be seasoned before cooking, but every chef has a different view on whether the same applies to meat. As a general rule at Daphne's meat is seasoned before cooking, unless it is required to have presentation marks on it from a grill (because seasoning draws out moisture, the meat won't mark so clearly). Meat grilled in this way is usually sliced after cooking and then seasoned with sea salt and freshly ground black pepper just before serving. When cooking vegetables it is best not to season them until they begin to soften, or the salt can't penetrate properly. Season mushrooms, in particular, before cooking and they will harden, as will chickpeas and beans. Most sauces made from good stock shouldn't need seasoning.

# Pecorino

Made with ewe's milk, Pecorino cheese, with its clean, salty flavour, is frequently soft when young, becoming hard when it is pressed and matured. The restaurant uses eight-month-old Pecorino Fiori Sardo, made from the milk of an ancient breed of sheep in the mountains of Sardinia. Much of the cheese is still made in farmhouses, rather than factories, and hand-finished with olive oil and ewe's suet rubbed into the skin to seal in moisture and prevent surface mould. Its distinctive flavour, not unlike that of Parmesan, can instantly lift pasta, salads or polenta.

# basil

Basil will go black quickly if bruised from rough chopping so either tear it or use a very sharp knife if cutting. Always pick and chop or tear basil as required; if it is cut too early it will quickly start to lose its flavour. Basil makes a dramatic flavouring for mashed potato. Blanch it first very briefly in boiling water, then refresh it in cold water to retain its intense green colour, chop it and mix it into some softened butter and beat it into the potatoes. Basil oil for drizzling over fish or vegetables can be made by adding basil stalks and black peppercorns to olive oil, and letting it infuse for an hour or so in a bain-marie (see oils, page 10) before bottling in sterilised jars.

# buffalo mozzarella

Like buffalo ricotta, buffalo mozzarella has a strength of flavour that the cow's-milk variety lacks: creamy, slightly salty, almost grassy. In and around Naples you can order really fresh mozzarella that is only hours old. It is quite firm and elastic, is weighed and priced accordingly and served only with olive oil or perhaps some tomato and basil. That is the best way to serve the best buffalo mozzarella, as simply as possible, so that you can savour the delicate, milky taste.

# tomato, aubergine & basil compote

25ml/1fl oz *extra virgin olive oil*

75ml/3fl oz *vegetable oil*

300g/10oz *aubergines, cut into batons of any desired length or shape*

50ml/2fl oz *garlic oil* (see page 10)

125g/4oz *cherry tomatoes, cut in half*

10 *basil leaves*

*salt and freshly ground black pepper*

 *This compote makes an ideal accompaniment to most meat dishes (see beef tagliata, page 165). It can be made up to 24 hours in advance of serving.*

1 Heat the olive and vegetable oils together in a large frying pan until they begin to smoke.

2 Add the aubergine batons and cook until golden brown, about 3 minutes. Drain off the excess oil and reserve to use in another recipe if desired.

3 Heat the garlic oil in another frying pan and when it is almost smoking, after about 5 minutes, add the cherry tomato halves.

4 Place the aubergine batons in a large bowl. Season well, then tear basil leaves over the top. Pour the cherry tomato/garlic mixture on top of the basil.

5 Cover the bowl in plastic wrap and leave to infuse in a warm place for about 15 minutes.

6 Check the seasoning and serve immediately with grilled fish, poultry or meats. If you particularly like the taste of fresh basil, you can sprinkle some more torn leaves over the top of the compote just before serving.

# slow-roast tomatoes

12 *plum tomatoes, cut in half*

2 handfuls *herb stalks, such as basil, parsley, sage,*
*oregano, marjoram*

*extra virgin olive oil for drizzling*

*salt (optional, if savoury taste desired)*

1  Preheat oven to lowest possible temperature.
   Lay tomato halves on a baking tray, drizzle with
   olive oil, spread herb stalks over the tomatoes
   and sprinkle with salt if you prefer a savoury
   taste rather than a naturally sweet one.
2  Bake for 8-12 hours, then remove and allow
   to cool before using.

 *Slow-roast tomatoes make a flavoursome addition to*
*a green salad or a bowl of plain pasta — the longer*
*they are cooked the more intense their flavour.*
*Instead of buying herbs especially for this dish, save the stalks of*
*herbs such as oregano, parsley or sage, after using the leaves in*
*other dishes. Simply freeze the stalks until you want to use them.*

# vegetable stock

MAKES 1.25 LITRES/2 PINTS

1 *leek*

1 *onion*

1 *carrot*

2 *celery sticks*

1 tbsp *vegetable oil*

4 *black peppercorns*

1 *bay leaf*

1.5 litres/2½ pints *water*

*salt and freshly ground black pepper*

1   Remove the outer leaves from the leek and wash it thoroughly. Roughly chop all the vegetables.

2   Heat the oil in a large saucepan and add the vegetables, together with the peppercorns and bay leaf. Cook for 5 minutes, stirring occasionally, without colouring.

3   Stir in the cold water and bring the stock slowly to the boil. Reduce to a simmer and skim away any impurities.

4   Continue to cook the stock for 1½ hours. Leave to infuse for 24 hours if time allows, then strain the stock through a fine sieve.

5   Season and leave to cool. If not using immediately, store in a refrigerator for up to 3 days, or freeze in ice-cube trays.

# fish stock

MAKES 1.25 LITRES/2 PINTS

1 *leek*

1 *onion*

2 *celery sticks*

1 head of *fennel*

1kg/2lb *fish bones from flat white fish such as turbot, soaked in cold water to remove blood*

1 tbsp vegetable oil

1 *bay leaf*

4 *peppercorns*

100ml/3½fl oz *white wine*

1.5 litres/2½ pints *water*

*salt and freshly ground black pepper*

1   Remove the outer leaves from the leek and wash it thoroughly. Roughly chop all the vegetables and the fish bones.

2   Heat the oil in a large saucepan, place all ingredients except the wine, water and seasoning in the saucepan and cook without colouring for 3–4 minutes, stirring occasionally.

3   Deglaze the pan with the white wine, cover with cold water and bring to the boil. Reduce heat, skim away any impurities and simmer for 20 minutes.

4   Remove from the heat and strain the stock through a fine sieve.

5   Season and leave to cool. If not using immediately, store in a refrigerator for up to 3 days, or freeze in ice-cube trays.

# veal stock

MAKES 1.25 LITRES/2 PINTS

1 *leek*

1 *onion*

1 *carrot*

2 *celery sticks*

4 *garlic cloves*

1 tbsp *vegetable oil, plus extra for drizzling*

1 *bay leaf*

4 *peppercorns*

1kg/2lb *veal bones*

1 tbsp *tomato concentrate*

100ml/3½fl oz *red wine*

1.5 litres/2½ pints *water*

*salt and freshly ground black pepper*

1 Preheat oven to 190°C (375°F), Gas Mark 5. Remove the outer leaves from the leek and wash it thoroughly. Roughly chop all the vegetables and garlic and place in a roasting tin.

2 Drizzle vegetables with oil and add the bay leaf and peppercorns. Bake in the oven till browned, about 40 minutes. Roast the veal bones in a separate tin without oil for about 50 minutes.

3 Heat the tablespoon of oil in a large saucepan. Add the vegetables, veal bones and tomato concentrate. Cook over high heat, stirring, for 2 minutes, then stir in the red wine.

4 Cover the mixture with cold water. Season, then bring to the boil and skim away any impurities. Reduce the heat and gently simmer for 1½–2 hours.

5 Strain the stock through a fine sieve. Season and leave to cool. If not using immediately, store in a refrigerator for up to 3 days, or freeze in ice-cube trays.

# chicken stock

MAKES 1.25 LITRES/2 PINTS

1 *leek*

1 *onion*

1 *carrot*

2 *celery sticks*

1kg/2lb *chicken bones*

1 tbsp *vegetable oil*

4 *black peppercorns*

1 *bay leaf*

1.5 litres/2½ pints *water*

*salt and freshly ground black pepper*

1 Remove the outer leaves from the leek and wash it thoroughly. Roughly chop all the vegetables and the chicken bones.

2 Heat the oil in a large saucepan and place all the ingredients in except the water and seasoning. Cook for 5 minutes, without allowing ingredients to colour, stirring occasionally.

3 Add the cold water and bring the stock to the boil. Reduce to a simmer and skim away any impurities. Continue to cook the stock for 1½–2 hours.

4 Strain the stock through a fine sieve. Season and leave to cool. If not using immediately, store in a refrigerator for up to 3 days, or freeze in ice-cube trays.

# cannellini beans in stock

200g/7oz *dried cannellini beans, soaked overnight*

50ml/2fl oz *extra virgin olive oil*

50g/2oz *prosciutto hock*

2–3 *garlic cloves, crushed*

1 litre/1¼ pints *vegetable stock* (see page 20)

1 *carrot*

2 *celery sticks*

1 *leek*

1 *onion, cut into quarters*

1 *bay leaf*

2 sprigs each *thyme or rosemary*

*salt and freshly ground black pepper*

1  Rinse the cannellini beans in cold water.

2  Heat the oil in a large saucepan and add the prosciutto and garlic. Sauté for 1 minute to flavour the oil.

3  Add the cannellini beans and sauté for a further 2 minutes, then pour in the vegetable stock, stirring all the time.

4  Cut the vegetables into large pieces and use string to tie them together with the bay leaf and herb sprigs to make a bouquet garni. Place it carefully in the stock.

5  Bring the stock to the boil, skim off any impurities, then simmer over low heat for 1½–2 hours, until the beans begin to burst open.

6  Season well, then remove bouquet garni and leave the beans to cool in the liquid.

 *Whenever you cook dried beans remember not to salt the water at the beginning of cooking, always at the end, or the skins will harden.*

# mustard dressing

MAKES 600ML/1 PINT

5 tbsps *Dijon mustard*

2 tbsps *red wine vinegar*

250ml/8fl oz *extra virgin olive oil*

250ml/8fl oz *vegetable oil*

*salt and freshly ground black pepper*

1 In a large bowl, mix the mustard and the red wine vinegar together.

2 Whisk in the oils slowly, a little at a time, until the dressing is combined.

3 Season to taste. If not using immediately, keep covered in the refrigerator for up to 10 days.

# lemon & olive oil dressing

MAKES 750ML/1¼ PINTS

175ml/6fl oz *lemon juice, freshly squeezed*

575ml/18fl oz *extra virgin olive oil*

*salt and freshly ground black pepper*

1 Pour the lemon juice into a bowl and whisk in the olive oil slowly, a little at a time, until the dressing is combined.

2 Season well. If not using immediately, keep covered in the refrigerator for up to 6 months.

# red wine vinegar dressing

MAKES 925ML/1½ PINTS

275ml/9fl oz *red wine vinegar*

575ml/18fl oz *extra virgin olive oil*

75ml/3fl oz *vegetable oil*

*salt and freshly ground black pepper*

1 Pour the red wine vinegar into a large bowl and whisk in the oils slowly, a little at a time, until the dressing is combined.

2 Season well. If not using immediately, keep covered in the refrigerator for up to 6 months.

# tomato sauce

MAKES 1.25 LITRES/2 PINTS

2 *garlic cloves*

275ml/9fl oz *extra virgin olive oil*

500g/1lb *plum tomatoes, ripe from the vine*

575ml/18fl oz *vegetable stock* (see page 20)

*salt and freshly ground black pepper*

1 Peel and chop the garlic and place it in a large saucepan with the olive oil. Cook slowly, stirring occasionally, for 2–3 minutes.
2 Roughly chop the tomatoes and add them to the saucepan, stirring. Season well and cook for 3 minutes.
3 Add the vegetable stock to the pan, stir and slowly bring to the boil. Cook over a low simmer, stirring occasionally, for 30 minutes.
4 Season and leave to cool. If not using immediately, keep covered in a refrigerator for up to 4 days.

# basil mayonnaise

1 *egg yolk*

30g/1¼oz *shallots, peeled and finely chopped*

1 tsp *white wine vinegar*

1 *garlic clove, crushed*

15g/½oz *anchovies, tinned or salted*

1 tsp *Dijon mustard*

200ml/7fl oz *vegetable oil*

100ml/3½fl oz *extra virgin olive oil*

125g/4oz *basil, finely chopped*

*salt and freshly ground black pepper*

1 Place the egg yolk, shallots, white wine vinegar, garlic, anchovies and mustard in the bowl of a food processor fitted with the metal blade. Whiz together until all the ingredients have emulsified, about 2 minutes.
2 Slowly add the vegetable oil and then the olive oil to the mayonnaise, stirring all the time. Finally, stir in the basil, season and transfer to a serving bowl. Refrigerate until needed.

 *A cherry tomato infusion makes an alternative tomato sauce for pasta dishes. Heat 150ml/¼ pint of olive oil in a pan with 2 crushed garlic cloves and a few sprigs of rosemary and thyme over a low heat for 10 minutes. Allow to cool and transfer to a large bowl. Add 500g/1lb of cherry tomatoes, halved, and season. Keeps for up to 4 days.*

# anchovy & olive salsa

MAKES 1 LITRE/1¾ PINTS

125g/4oz *anchovies*

50g/2oz *shallots*

4 *garlic cloves*

1 bunch each *parsley and oregano*

12 *mint leaves*

125g/4oz *black olives, pitted*

50g/2oz *capers, rinsed well*

1 litre/1¾ pints *extra virgin olive oil*

1  On a chopping board, finely chop the anchovies, shallots and garlic almost to a paste. Transfer to a large bowl.

2  Finely chop the parsley, oregano and mint together. Add to the bowl.

3  Roughly chop the black olives and capers (this adds a little texture to the salsa). Add them to the bowl.

4  Pour in the olive oil, then mix all the ingredients together carefully. Cover with plastic wrap and leave in a warm place to infuse for about 20 minutes.

5  If not using immediately, keep covered in a refrigerator for up to 4 days.

# pesto

MAKES 200G/7OZ

1 bunch *basil*

½ bunch *parsley*

50g/2oz *salted capers, rinsed*

50g/2oz *pine nuts, toasted* (see page 13)

2 *garlic cloves*

275ml/9fl oz *extra virgin olive oil*

50g/2oz *freshly grated Parmesan*

*salt and freshly ground black pepper*

1  Coarsely chop the herbs, capers and garlic and transfer to a mortar. Add the olive oil, Parmesan and seasoning and grind with a pestle until the pesto reaches a rough consistency.

2  If not using immediately, keep covered in a refrigerator for up to 3 days.

 *This salsa is great not just with pasta but over grilled meat or fish. Feel free to adjust the proportion of anchovies and olives to suit your taste.*

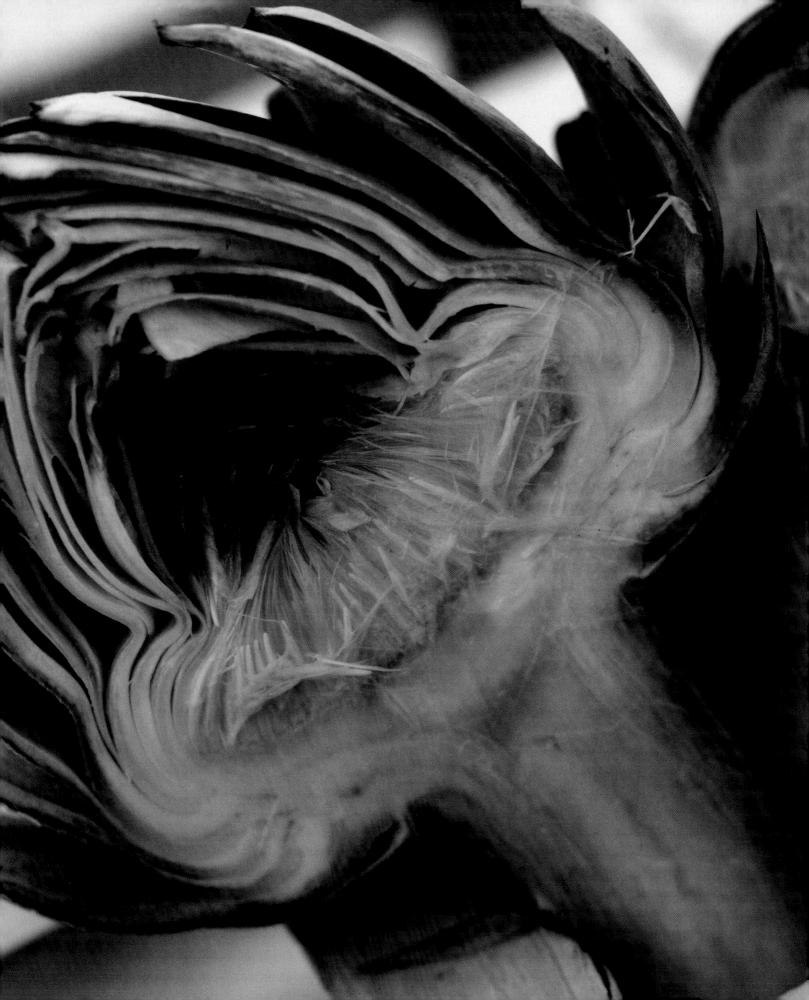

# vegetables

wild mushroom bruschetta

potato, Provolone & pancetta

prosciutto with figs

asparagus with Hollandaise in a Parmesan basket

Caesar salad

wild mushroom & ricotta tarts

fennel & orange salad

chargrilled vegetable salad

sautéed porcini

baby spinach, avocado & crispy pancetta salad

endive, pear, Pecorino & walnut salad

aubergine & goat's cheese galettes

goat's cheese, pepper, radicchio & pine nut salad

zucchini fritti

porcini & rosemary soup

bruschetta with borlotti purée,
    goat's cheese & walnuts

 THINK OF A TYPICAL ITALIAN MARKET WITH ITS DISPLAYS OF RIPE TOMATOES, FLUTTERY GOLDEN COURGETTE FLOWERS, MINIATURE ARTICHOKES, SHINY AUBERGINES, RADICCHIO AND WILD ROCKET. THESE ARE THE ESSENTIAL FLAVOURS FOR THE VEGETABLE BASKET …

# aubergines
Pale purple, slightly streaked aubergines are creamier and less bitter than the more usual deep-purple ones, and they work well in dishes in which the vegetable is cooked for some time. Because these pale aubergines have quite an open texture, however, they don't hold together so well on the grill, which is where the darker aubergines come into their own. Some people prefer to salt aubergines before use, to draw out any bitterness; at Daphne's the philosophy is that a salted aubergine tastes salty and the process is unnecessary.

# wild rocket
These days wild rocket is, of course, cultivated, but when people refer to wild rocket, they mean the original fine-leaved plant that used to grow wild in every hedgerow, with its bright colour and beautifully peppery flavour, rather than the larger-leaved variety, whose taste and texture pale next to it. The difference is as marked as that between curly and flat-leaf parsley. A simple salad of good wild rocket and Parmesan is a wonderful thing. Rocket also makes a good pesto-like salsa for serving with beef carpaccio or grilled fish. Just blend the rocket with some anchovies, capers, a little basil, mint and olive oil (not Tuscan, in this case, as that would add too much pepper), adding lemon juice right at the last minute. Scallops pan-fried with some chopped shallots and girolles are also delicious with wild rocket tossed in at the last minute, again with a squeeze of lemon. It can be added to a pasta sauce right at the end of cooking time, so that it wilts only slightly, or put in earlier and stewed down into a more wintery sauce, when it takes on a more mellow flavour that is delicious finished with a dash of truffle oil.

# plum tomatoes It isn't always easy to find the kind of fantastic super-ripe tomatoes you seem to see in every market in Italy that need little more than some salt and olive oil to bring out their intense flavour. Small cherry tomatoes on the vine are often the best bet. When you remove the stalk of the best tomatoes the aroma is reminiscent of a greenhouse, and the pips are slightly green and fresh-tasting. At Daphne's cherry tomatoes are used to make a chunky vibrant sauce for pasta (see box, page 25). Another version of this sauce is made using a mound of cherry tomatoes, which are halved, then put into hot olive oil in a hot pan so that they sizzle for about 30 seconds. They are tossed in the pan, so that the juices start coming out, and seasoned. A little chopped garlic is then added (don't put this in before the tomatoes, otherwise it will burn). As the tomatoes start to bubble and reduce very slightly, some torn basil leaves are thrown in, and a dash of extra virgin olive oil is added at the end.

In winter a good way of concentrating the flavour of plum tomatoes which may not be as flavoursome is to slow-bake them until they are dried and firm on the outside, but soft on the inside (see page 18). Then you can use them with grilled fish, chopped and mixed into a sauce (particularly good with lamb), or in a relish with fresh sage, some chopped onions (sweated in a little olive oil), some pitted black olives and basil. For a more liquid tomato sauce with plum tomatoes, try the recipe on page 25. Tomato passata (a purée of skinned, de-seeded tomatoes), which can be bought ready-made in tins from a delicatessen, is often added to sauces and casseroles to deepen the flavours. If unavailable, substitute with tinned plum tomatoes, puréed and passed through a sieve.

# pumpkin The pumpkin favoured at Daphne's is one used in Italy known as Iron Bark. It is a large, rock-hard pumpkin with a rough, knobbly rusty-orange-coloured skin and orange flesh. It can be cut into segments and roasted slowly, still with the skin on, for serving as an accompaniment to grilled meat, or the flesh can be puréed to make a soup or a sauce to go with gnocchi (see page 89).

# artichokes When you buy globe artichokes make sure they feel heavy and that the leaves look fresh and tightly closed. Trimming a globe artichoke is quite a complicated business, so even if you want to cook just the hearts, say to make mash, it is easier to boil the whole artichoke, then strip off the leaves and cut away the hairy choke, leaving just the base, or heart. The hearts can then be mashed, mixed in a ratio of 50:50 with mashed potato, and seasoned with lemon juice and olive oil, a little chopped garlic and lots of flat-leaf parsley. They can also be put into stews with peas, mint, pancetta, speck or lamb. If you are making more of a feature of the cooked heart, they are best simmered gently in a pan with part olive oil, part vegetable stock (if you like you can add a bay leaf and some garlic).

Always season artichokes well at the beginning of cooking, particularly with salt, as they are such densely textured vegetables they will absorb salt properly only when warm. The traditional French way of preparing artichokes is to cook them in a *blanc*, a mix of flour and water, which acts as an air barrier and helps the artichokes to cook more quickly. But cooking with oil and stock has the same effect, with the added benefit that you can store the artichokes, covered in this liquid, in the fridge.

Baby artichokes still on their stalks, the best being the spiky Italian spinosi, can be sliced lengthways and cooked in the same way, then used as a garnish for coppa, cut in half and chargrilled with lemon and olive oil, or deep-fried, either as they are or first dipped in milk then flour to form a light batter. Since they are still attached to the stalk, and therefore kept moist, these artichokes can also be shaved raw — along with Parmesan, a drizzling of lemon juice and oil — over beef carpaccio, though they may be a little bitter for some tastes.

# chard
Braised chard marries well with chargrilled fish and is also good added to casseroles with artichokes. Look for really fresh, crisp chard with bright-green leaves. Tender baby chard can be cooked whole, but when using large chard always separate the stalks from the leaves before cooking, as the stalks need more time. Braise the stalks in some white wine, vegetable stock and olive oil, with a dash of lemon juice to keep them white, and perhaps a bay leaf or some rosemary, then add the leaves at the last minute.

# courgette flowers
In Italian markets mounds of delicately flavoured, golden courgette, or zucchini, flowers are sold quite cheaply for adding liberally to risottos, salads and pasta. Unfortunately, by the time they are flown abroad, they inevitably become much more expensive, and are treated as a delicacy. The female flowers, which are the most costly, have a fruit attached and their flowers are more closed up than the cheaper, more open male flowers. The courgette fruit from the female flowers can be chopped into discs for putting into risottos, and the flowers added at the finish along with butter and Parmesan. The raw fruit can also be sliced finely into salads, along with the flowers and a dressing of lemon juice and olive oil, or the flowers may be stuffed with mozzarella, anchovy and basil and deep-fried.

# wild mushrooms
Wild mushrooms are a passion at Daphne's, with porcini, girolles, trompette de la mort, chanterelles and pied de mouton all used in risottos or cooked down with cream, garlic and shallots for serving on bruschetta (see page 38). For most people, the king of wild mushrooms is the porcino, which is the *Boletus edulus*, rather than the paler *Boletus badius*, or *bay bolete*, a close relative, whose flavour is not so intense. Usually the darker the caps of the porcini, the deeper their flavour. Good porcini should feel quite heavy, with no sign of maggots. Even so, they should be prepared carefully in case there are any inside. At Daphne's porcini are always used fresh, rather than dried, and are cooked really simply, either chargrilled or pan-fried, with a little garlic, parsley and olive oil (see page 50), added to risotto or pasta, shaved raw onto beef carpaccio, or made

into a hearty soup with rosemary (see page 59). When it comes to cleaning, there is a big debate as to whether to brush or wash mushrooms. A gritty mushroom is worse than a little extra moisture, so the best answer is probably to rinse the mushrooms thoroughly and then quickly and carefully dry them.

# radicchio Because radicchio has a bitter flavour it is best used sparingly. Of all the varieties

in the radicchio family Trevise, or radicchio rosso di Treviso, grown around Venice and Treviso, is one of the best. It has a slight sweetness, and a big broad stem with quite a lot of veining in the leaves. Trevise is excellent chargrilled, though grilling intensifies the bitterness and needs to be balanced with a dressing made from a little balsamic vinegar and extra virgin olive oil. Like rocket (see page 30) it can also be allowed to cook down a little in risottos or pasta sauces, so that it takes on a nutty flavour.

# white truffles The white truffle from Alba (*Tuber magnatum*) is more highly perfumed

than the black truffle (*Tuber melanosporum*), with a glorious, pungent and definitely acquired taste. The first fabulously expensive white truffles begin to arrive in October and are carefully weighed in the restaurant kitchen. Ideally they should be golf ball-sized and not at all spongy, which would show that the truffle is old. In the season (until about January) a heady aroma fills the restaurant when a great ceremony is made of shaving white truffles at the customers table, especially over the delicate white truffle risotto made with light chicken stock, finished with butter and the shaved truffles. One of the simplest luxuries is to grate a little fresh truffle over scrambled eggs or melted cheese on toast.

# fennel The female fennel is round and bulbous, juicy, creamier and more mellow, less intensely

aniseedy than the straighter, flatter male version. Serve it raw in the classic Sicilian salad with oranges (see page 47), chargrill it and serve with orange oil (see page 10), or slice it into segments and pan-fry in olive oil, then sprinkle with salt and pepper, transfer it to a medium oven and cook until it caramelises and dries slightly on the outside, but is melting inside. Cooked that way it is wonderful with fish. You could also make a soup by cooking the sliced fennel in milk then puréeing it with lots of olive oil. Pass it through a sieve and finally add plenty of salt and black pepper. When fennel is cooked in this way, slowly, with a creamy ingredient, the aniseed gives way to something sweeter, in the same way that roast carrot takes on a sweetness that the raw vegetable doesn't have.

# fava beans There isn't anything quite like the first fresh, young fava, or broad, beans of

the season, which make a wonderful risotto with ham hocks, and are delicious in salads with Pecorino, lemon and olive oil, or in stews with artichokes. Like peas, they freeze well. At Daphne's fresh fava beans are used when in season, though they can be bought dried or frozen.

# wild mushroom bruschetta

| |
|---|
| 4 slices *ciabatta bread, about 4cm/1½in thick* |
| 50ml/2fl oz *extra virgin olive oil* |
| 50g/2oz *butter* |
| 300g/10oz *mixed wild mushrooms, such as porcini, chanterelles, girolles, pied bleu, trompette de la mort* |
| 50g/2oz *shallots, finely diced* |
| 2 *garlic cloves, crushed with salt to a purée* |
| 50ml/2fl oz *Marsala* |
| 100ml/3½fl oz *chicken stock* (see page 21) |
| 100ml/3½fl oz *double cream* |
| ½ bunch *flat-leaf parsley* |
| *salt and freshly ground black pepper* |

1  Preheat oven to a very low temperature, about 110°C (225°F), Gas Mark ¼. Then preheat the grill and lightly toast or chargrill the ciabatta slices on both sides.

2  Place the ciabatta on a baking tray. Drizzle with olive oil and bake in the oven for about 20 minutes until golden and crispy.

3  Melt a knob of butter in a large frying pan. Add your first choice of mushroom and sauté until soft, about 3 minutes. Season well. Fry each of the mushroom types separately in the same frying pan and leave to drain in a colander, reserving the stock from the mushrooms.

4  When the last variety of mushroom is cooked, melt another knob of butter in the frying pan. Add the shallots and garlic purée. Sauté until the shallots are soft, about 4 minutes.

5  Deglaze the frying pan with Marsala, then reduce the liquid to about two-thirds. Add the chicken stock and the stock from the mushrooms and bring to the boil, stirring frequently.

6  Remove the frying pan from the heat and stir in the cream. Bring to the boil, then reduce the liquid to about one-fifth. Add the wild mushrooms and simmer for a further 5 minutes. Meanwhile, roughly chop the parsley.

7  Check the consistency (it should be moist enough to bind the mushrooms together but not too watery) and season.

8  Sprinkle the sauce with parsley, and serve immediately on top of individual ciabatta slices.

• *Serve with a light Italian Soave.*

# potato, Provolone & pancetta

400g/13oz *potatoes, King Edwards or Marfone*

40g/1½oz *pancetta*

125g/4oz *Provolone, Cacio Silano Bianco (if available)*

20 *sage leaves*

*extra virgin olive oil for drizzling*

*salt and freshly ground black pepper*

1 Boil the potatoes in their skins in a saucepan full of salted water, then simmer until they are about three-quarters cooked, about 30 minutes. Remove the potatoes from the liquid and leave to cool in a colander.

2 Preheat oven to 180°C (350°F), Gas Mark 4.

3 Meanwhile, slice the potatoes, pancetta and Provolone thinly and layer alternately in a shallow heatproof serving dish. Place a sage leaf in between the potato and Provolone slices (allowing about 5 leaves per portion).

4 Season and add a drizzle of olive oil.

5 Bake in the oven for about 7–8 minutes until the Provolone has melted and is golden brown.

• *Serve with Sauvignon Blanc.*

*Provolone is an Italian curd cheese made from cow's milk, which is softened in hot water and shaped, then tied with string and hung to dry.*

# prosciutto with figs

400g/13oz *prosciutto, ideally Prosciutto di Parma*

125g/4oz *rocket, freshly picked (if possible)*

dash of *extra virgin olive oil*

4 *figs*

*freshly ground black pepper*

1  Slice the prosciutto very thinly and arrange it
   around a serving plate.
2  In a bowl, toss the rocket with a splash of
   olive oil and place it in the centre of each plate.
3  Cut each fig into eighths and arrange them
   on top of the prosciutto. Finish with a twist
   of black pepper and serve immediately.

• *Serve with Pinot Grigio.*

*Try to buy prosciutto that is sliced in front of you
at the delicatessen, rather than pre-packed. Once
sliced it rapidly dries out, losing its succulence.*

# asparagus with Hollandaise in a Parmesan basket

600g/1¼lb *asparagus*

50g/2oz *freshly grated Parmesan*

100 ml/3⅓fl oz *white wine*

50 ml/2fl oz *white wine vinegar*

250g/8oz *butter*

2 *egg yolks, beaten*

1 Blanch the asparagus in boiling water for about 3 minutes, then remove and place in iced water.

2 Preheat oven to 180°C (350°F), Gas Mark 4. On a non-stick baking tray arrange the grated Parmesan into 4 x 10cm/4in discs, filling a circular cookie cutter with enough cheese to cover the bottom of the tray. Cook in the oven for 8 minutes until lightly brown, then remove and mould each disc over an upturned cup and leave to cool there to form a basket.

3 For the Hollandaise sauce, boil the white wine and white wine vinegar in a pan until reduced by half, about 4 minutes. Allow to cool.

4 Melt the butter in a pan or in the microwave. Allow to cool, then ladle out the sediment.

5 Place the egg yolks and wine reduction into a metal bowl and place over a pan of boiling water. Whisk continually until it reaches a thick consistency, about 5-6 minutes, then add the clarified butter very slowly. (If the sauce gets too thick add a little boiling water.)

6 To serve, spoon some Hollandaise sauce into the bottom of each Parmesan basket and place asparagus spears across the top of the basket.

• *Serve with Soave Classico.*

# Caesar salad

4 small *baby gem lettuces*

1 small *baguette*

*vegetable oil for frying*

25g/1oz *freshly grated Parmesan*

125g/4oz *Parmesan block*

*salt and freshly ground black pepper*

**for the dressing**

1 large *shallot*

1 *garlic clove*

30g/1¼oz *tinned anchovies*

25g/1oz *freshly grated Parmesan*

2 *egg yolks*

juice of 2 *lemons*

dash of *Tabasco sauce*

dash of *Worcestershire sauce*

275ml/9fl oz *vegetable oil*

*warm water (optional)*

1 To make the dressing, place all the ingredients except the vegetable oil and water in the bowl of a food processor fitted with the metal blade.

2 Whiz until smooth, then slowly add the vegetable oil until you have a smooth, thick dressing. If the dressing becomes too thick, add a little warm water.

3 Remove the core from the baby gem lettuces, wash the leaves thoroughly and leave to drain in a colander. Then cut the leaves roughly into bite-sized strips.

4 For the croûtons, dice the baguette into 5mm/¼in pieces. In a deep-fat fryer, heat the oil to 180°C (350°F). Deep-fry the bread until golden brown, about 3 minutes. Drain on kitchen paper, then salt well and sprinkle grated Parmesan over the top.

5 To serve, mix the lettuce and croûtons together in a bowl with the dressing. Transfer to 4 plates. With a vegetable peeler, shave the Parmesan block and arrange the shavings on top of the salad. Finish with freshly ground black pepper.

• *Serve with Californian Chardonnay.*

# wild mushroom & ricotta tarts

4 x 6cm/2½in *shortcrust pastry tart cases, baked blind*

**for the filling**

1 *onion*

2 *garlic cloves*

100ml/3½fl oz *extra virgin olive oil*

2 *rosemary sprigs, leaves picked and finely chopped*

125g/4oz *mixed wild mushrooms, such as mousserons, porcini, girolles, pied bleu, finely chopped*

25ml/1fl oz *white wine*

35g/1½oz *mascarpone*

200ml/7fl oz *double cream*

60g/2½oz *ricotta*

2 *eggs, beaten*

*butter for greasing*

30g/1½oz *freshly grated Parmesan*

*salt and freshly ground black pepper*

**for the garnish**

15ml/½fl oz *truffle oil*

60g/2½oz *wild rocket*

1  Preheat oven to 180°C (350°F), Gas Mark 4.

2  To make the filling, peel and finely chop the onion and garlic. Heat the olive oil in a frying pan and slowly cook the onion and garlic together with the rosemary for 2–3 minutes.

3  Add the mushrooms and continue cooking for 4 minutes. Then pour in the white wine and cook until reduced by half.

4  Next, remove the pan from the heat to add the mascarpone and double cream. Return pan to the heat and, again, cook to reduce by half. Then remove the pan from the heat and mix in the ricotta.

5  Allow the filling to cool for about an hour. When cool, transfer it to a bowl. Add the eggs and season.

6  Place the pre-baked pastry cases on a greased baking sheet. Pour the filling into the cases and sprinkle Parmesan on top of the tarts. Bake in the oven until firm to the touch, about 20 minutes.

7  In a bowl mix half of the truffle oil with the rocket and season to taste. Place individual tarts on small serving plates, drizzle the tops with the remaining truffle oil and garnish with rocket.

• *Serve with Sauvignon Blanc.*

# fennel & orange salad

4 large *oranges*

100ml/3½fl oz *extra virgin olive oil*

50ml/2fl oz *orange juice, freshly squeezed if possible*

4 small heads of *fennel*

*salt and freshly ground black pepper*

**for the dressing**

150g/5oz *wild rocket*

100ml/3½fl oz *extra virgin olive oil*

25ml/1fl oz *orange juice, freshly squeezed if possible*

**for the garnish**

80g/3¼oz *wild rocket*

1  Marinate the oranges a day in advance of serving the salad. To do this, peel and segment the oranges. Place them on a tray and season well. Pour olive oil and orange juice over the top and leave the oranges in the refrigerator, covered, for 24 hours.

2  To prepare the fennel, trim the tops from the fennel heads and cut each into eight wedges. Remove most of the root from each one, being careful to leave enough on the fennel to hold the wedges together, and set aside.

3  For the dressing, put the rocket and olive oil in the bowl of a food processor fitted with the metal blade. Whiz until smooth, about 3 minutes, and season well.

4  To serve the salad, place the rocket garnish on individual plates and arrange the fennel and orange segments in a stack on top. In a bowl, mix the orange juice with the rocket dressing and drizzle it over the top of each salad.

• *Serve with Pouilly Fumé.*

# chargrilled vegetable salad

1 head of *fennel, trimmed*

60g/2½oz *white asparagus, peeled and trimmed*

1 *aubergine, trimmed and cut in half lengthways*

1 *yellow courgette*

1 *red pepper*

200ml/7fl oz *extra virgin olive oil,*

*plus extra for drizzling*

15g/½oz *tinned anchovies, chopped*

2 *garlic cloves, finely chopped*

2 *thyme sprigs, leaves picked and roughly chopped*

zest of ½ *orange*

4 *basil leaves*

dash of *white wine vinegar*

300g/10oz *cherry tomatoes*

25ml/1fl oz *white wine*

*salt and freshly ground black pepper*

1  Preheat oven to 200°C (400°F), Gas Mark 6.

2  Cut the fennel into 8 wedges and blanch in a saucepan of boiling, salted water until al dente. Remove the fennel with a slotted spoon and transfer to a bowl of iced water; set aside.

3  Blanch the white asparagus as for the fennel. Slice the aubergine halves into 5mm/¼in pieces. Slice the courgette into 5mm/¼in rings.

4  Drizzle the pepper with a little oil and roast in the oven for 30–40 minutes until just blackened. Allow to cool slightly and peel the skin. Reduce oven heat to 150°C (300°F), Gas Mark 2.

5  Chargrill all the prepared vegetables on a griddle pan or grill plate for 2–3 minutes, marking them well on both sides. Place the vegetables in separate bowls, season well and add 25ml/1fl oz olive oil to each bowl.

6  Add the anchovies to the aubergines and add half the garlic to the courgettes. Then add half the thyme to the pepper and add orange zest to the fennel. Add 2 basil leaves and a dash of white wine vinegar to the asparagus.

7  Place the cherry tomatoes in a deep oven tray with the remaining thyme, the remaining garlic, the white wine and 50ml/2fl oz olive oil. Cover with foil and bake in the oven for about 20 minutes until they are starting to split open.

8  To serve, drain the oil away from the vegetables, reserving it in a separate bowl. Heat the vegetables through in the oven for about 6–8 minutes, and arrange them on a warm serving platter. Finally, tear and scatter the remaining basil leaves on top of the vegetables and drizzle with a little of the reserved oil.

• *Serve with Californian Chardonnay.*

# baby spinach, avocado & crispy pancetta salad

*125g/4oz baguette, cut into 5mm/¼in dice*

*vegetable oil for deep-frying*

*25g/1oz freshly grated Parmesan*

*oil for greasing baking sheet*

*50g/2oz pancetta, very thinly sliced*

*2 large avocados*

*150g/5oz baby spinach, freshly picked (if possible) and washed*

*100ml/3½fl oz mustard dressing (see page 24)*

*salt and freshly ground black pepper*

1 Preheat oven to 180°C (350°F), Gas Mark 4. Meanwhile, make croûtons from the baguette (see Caesar salad, page 45).

2 Place the pancetta on a greased baking sheet and bake in the oven until brown and crispy, about 10 minutes. Allow to cool.

3 Halve, peel and slice the avocados. Season well.

4 In a bowl, mix together the baby spinach, half of the crispy pancetta, the croûtons, avocado and two-thirds of the dressing. Season.

5 To serve, arrange the salad on serving plates. Place the remaining pancetta on top of each salad and drizzle the remaining dressing over the top.

• *Serve with Sancerre.*

# sautéed porcini

*200ml/7fl oz garlic oil (see page 10)*

*600g/1¼lb fresh porcini, sliced*

*50g/2oz flat-leaf parsley, finely shredded*

*salt and freshly ground black pepper*

1 Heat the oil in a frying pan and fry the porcini until golden brown, about 6 minutes, shaking the pan occasionally.

2 Season to taste. Add the parsley to the mixture and toss the pan until the ingredients are combined.

• *Serve with Barolo.*

# endive, pear, Pecorino & walnut salad

4 medium *endive*

½ head of *radicchio, stalk removed*

50g/2oz *Pecorino*

1 *pear*

25g/1oz *watercress, freshly picked (if possible)*

60g/2½oz *freshly peeled walnuts*

65ml/2½fl oz *red wine vinegar dressing* (see page 24)

*salt and freshly ground black pepper*

1 Take 12 attractive leaves from the endive and reserve them for use later on. Thinly slice the remaining endive and the radicchio.

2 Cut the Pecorino into dice of about 5mm/¼in. Then cut the pear into quarters. Remove the core and slice thinly.

3 Mix all the above ingredients, together with the watercress and walnuts, in a large bowl. Add the dressing, reserving a little, and season.

4 To serve, toss the reserved endive leaves in the remaining dressing and season. Arrange 3 leaves in a triangle on each serving plate and heap the salad on top.

• *Serve with Chardonnay or Sauvignon Blanc.*

# aubergine & goat's cheese galettes

*for the galettes*

plain flour for rolling out

250g/8oz *puff pastry*

butter for greasing

*for the filling*

100ml/3½fl oz *extra virgin olive oil, plus extra for drizzling*

4 medium *aubergines, peeled and cut into small cubes*

2 *garlic cloves, peeled and finely chopped*

2 *thyme sprigs*

2 *rosemary sprigs*

150g/5oz *goat's cheese*

salt and freshly ground black pepper

*for the topping*

8 *medium tomatoes, thinly sliced*

1 *red onion, thinly sliced and cut into small pieces*

16 *black olives, pitted and cut in half*

8 *fresh basil leaves*

*for the garnish*

125g/4oz *wild rocket*

50ml/2fl oz *extra virgin olive oil*

1 Preheat oven to 200°C (400°F), Gas Mark 6. Meanwhile, on a floured surface, roll the puff pastry out to a thickness of about 3mm/⅛in. From this, cut out 4 x 6cm/2½in discs and place them on a greased baking sheet. Bake until golden brown, about 20 minutes, then remove from oven. Keep the oven on at the same temperature.

2 Meanwhile, to make the filling, heat the olive oil in a frying pan, add the diced aubergines, garlic and herbs and fry very slowly until the aubergine is almost a purée.

3 Remove the herbs from the frying pan and add the goat's cheese. Mix it in well and season to taste. Spread the filling over the top of the galettes.

4 Place the tomato slices in a ring around the edge of each galette. Sprinkle a few pieces of red onion over the top of the tomatoes

5 Place a few olives and 2 basil leaves on top of each galette. Season well. Drizzle olive oil over each one and return to the oven for 5 minutes or until hot.

6 For the garnish, mix the rocket with the olive oil in a bowl and season to taste. To serve, place each galette on a plate and top with the rocket.

• *Serve with Rosé de Provence.*

# goat's cheese, pepper, radicchio & pine nut salad

3 *yellow peppers, cut in half lengthwise, deseeded and cored*

2 tbsps *extra virgin olive oil, plus extra for drizzling*

6 large *plum tomatoes, quartered and deseeded*

2 large handfuls *rocket*

1 *radicchio, stalk removed*

1 tbsp *red wine vinegar*

250g/8oz *soft goat's cheese log, sliced into 12 circles*

1 large handful *black olives, pitted*

1 tbsp *pine nuts, toasted (see page 13)*

½ bunch *basil*

*salt and freshly ground black pepper*

1  Preheat oven to 180°C (350°F), Gas Mark 4. Cut the peppers into about 24 triangles and lay them on an oiled baking sheet. Drizzle with olive oil and sprinkle with salt.

2  Place the tomatoes on an oiled baking sheet. Drizzle with olive oil and sprinkle with salt.

3  Place the 2 trays in the oven, baking the tomatoes for 35 minutes and the peppers for about 45 minutes, by which time they will be shrivelled, lightly browned and very tender. This will greatly intensify the flavour.

4  Leave the peppers and tomatoes to cool on the baking sheets. Meanwhile, finely shred the rocket and radicchio. Combine them together in a bowl and dress with 1 tablespoon of red wine vinegar and 2 tablespoons of olive oil.

5  Just before serving, place the goat's cheese on a tray and grill lightly, about 30 seconds.

6  Arrange 6 pieces of pepper and tomato on each plate to resemble a clockface. Place the salad in a pile in the middle of the peppers and place 3 pieces of goat's cheese in a circle on top. Scatter olives and pine nuts around the peppers and tomatoes. Then, using scissors, shred the basil over the goat's cheese and drizzle with olive oil. Season with black pepper.

• *Serve with Rosé de Provence.*

# zucchini fritti

6 courgettes (zucchini)

600ml/1 pint milk

50g/2oz plain flour

vegetable oil for deep-frying

salt and freshly ground black pepper

1  Cut the courgettes lengthwise into strips about 3mm/⅛in thick. Pour the milk into a shallow bowl and dip the courgettes in it.

2  Put the flour into a separate shallow bowl. Dip the courgettes in the flour and shake well to remove any excess flour.

3  In a deep-fat fryer, heat the oil to a temperature of 190°C (375°F) and deep-fry the courgettes until golden brown, about 3 minutes. Be careful not to shake the fryer too much or the courgettes will break into small pieces.

4  Remove the courgettes from the fryer and drain on kitchen paper. Season and serve immediately.

• Serve with Orvieto Classico.

# porcini & rosemary soup

125g/4oz butter

100ml/3½fl oz extra virgin olive oil

200g/7oz fresh porcini, sliced

2 garlic cloves, crushed with salt to a purée

50g/2oz onion, roughly chopped

50g/2oz celery, roughly chopped

50g leeks, outer leaves removed, washed
and roughly chopped

50g/2oz rosemary, leaves picked and finely chopped

400ml/14fl oz white wine

2 litres/3½ pints chicken stock (see page 21)

salt and freshly ground black pepper

1  In a large saucepan, heat the butter and oil together. When the mixture is hot, about 3 minutes, sauté the porcini until golden brown, about 6 minutes. Season well and remove from the saucepan; set aside.

2  Add the garlic purée, onion, celery, leeks and rosemary to the saucepan. Sauté for 5 minutes.

3  Next, pour in the white wine and reduce by four-fifths, until the alcohol has burnt out.

4  Add the chicken stock. Bring the soup to a boil, reduce the heat and return the porcini to the saucepan. Simmer for 30 minutes.

5  Check the seasoning and serve.

• Serve with Soave Classico.

 *The batter for the zucchini fritti is not only simple, it works much more effectively than heavier batters. Drizzle over some truffle oil at the end if you like.*

# bruschetta with borlotti purée, goat's cheese & walnuts

125g/4oz *borlotti beans, soaked overnight*

1 litre/1¼ pints *vegetable stock (see page 20)*

100ml/3½fl oz *extra virgin olive oil, plus extra for drizzling*

1 *garlic clove, crushed , plus half a whole clove to rub over the ciabatta*

several sprigs each *thyme or rosemary*

½ *red pepper, skin removed and deseeded*

dash of *red wine vinegar*

4 *slices ciabatta, about 3cm/1½in thick*

1 *radicchio*

75ml/3fl oz *balsamic vinegar, plus extra for drizzling*

160g/5½oz *goat's cheese*

125g/4oz *rocket, freshly picked (if possible)*

50ml/2fl oz *walnut oil*

20g/¾oz *fresh walnuts, skins removed and chopped*

salt and freshly ground black pepper

1 Cook the borlotti beans in vegetable stock with 50ml/2fl oz of olive oil, the crushed garlic and herbs as per cannellini beans in stock (see page 23). Meanwhile, preheat grill and preheat oven to lowest temperature.

2 When the beans are cooked, remove the herbs. Pour the mixture into the bowl of a food processor fitted with the metal blade. Add the red pepper and purée, about 3 minutes.

3 Add red wine vinegar and seasoning to taste.

4 Chargrill, or toast, the ciabatta on both sides, then rub with garlic, drizzle with olive oil and bake in the oven for about 20 minutes.

5 Meanwhile, cut the radicchio into quarters lengthwise, removing the root. Place leaves on a tray and drizzle with olive oil. Chargrill, or grill, the radicchio, about 2 minutes. When cooked, toss in a bowl with the balsamic vinegar and 50ml/2fl oz of olive oil. Check the seasoning and leave to infuse for about 45 minutes.

6 Place the ciabatta slices on a baking sheet. Spread each one with a layer of borlotti purée. Top with radicchio and then the goat's cheese. Bake in the oven for 7–8 minutes until the goat's cheese has just melted.

7 Meanwhile, in a bowl, toss the rocket in walnut oil, together with the walnuts and seasoning.

8 Arrange the rocket mixture around the edge of each plate. Place the ciabatta in the centre and drizzle balsamic vinegar around the plate.

• *Serve with Pinot Grigio.*

# pasta

basic pasta dough

pappardelle with rabbit

spaghetti seafood

salt cod & potato ravioli with clams
   & parsley

orecchiette with baked ricotta,
   wild greens & truffle oil

tagliolini with white truffle

scallop & rosemary ravioli

porcini & artichoke ravioli

garganelli with Parma ham, rocket,
   radicchio & pine nuts

penne with peppers, aubergine & mozzarella

linguini clams

salmon, spinach, rocket & ricotta rotolo

anolini nero with sea bass, saffron & tomato

lobster & fennel ravioli

penne with courgettes, walnuts & Pecorino

gnocchi

pumpkin gnocchi

SALT IS THE SECRET TO COOKING PASTA PERFECTLY, BECAUSE SALINATED WATER BOILS AT A HIGHER TEMPERATURE THAN PLAIN WATER. USE A GOOD TEASPOON PER LITRE OF WATER TO PRODUCE FIRMLY TEXTURED PASTA THAT WILL FORM THE BASE FOR COUNTLESS SIMPLE VARIATIONS.

pasta In Italy great store is set by what pasta goes with which sauce. It is all about texture and shape. The general rule is that a thin sauce requires hollow, more absorbent pasta than thicker sauces do. Chunky, rich sauces need chunky pasta like penne or rigatoni; thinner more delicate sauces, such as those made with vongole (clams), need to coat themselves around thin strands, so spaghetti, spaghettini and linguine are the obvious choices. Soft broad fresh pappardelle works well with rich, meatier sauces, such as rabbit (see page 66). Soft egg pasta, such as ravioli and other filled pasta, flat fettucine, tagliatelle (which is a little wider) and garganelle (ribbed rolls of pasta) are at their best fresh. Those made with durum wheat, like spaghetti and linguine, are better bought dried, as they are in Italy. (Don't try working with durum wheat flour at home as domestic pasta machines are not strong enough to cope with it.) It is worth paying a little more for good-quality, slightly rough-surfaced spaghetti, rather than very smooth, shiny pasta that will have no real bite to it and won't cling as well to the sauce. The other classic pasta used at Daphne's is orecchiette (little ears), handmade with flour and water, whose shape grips well onto a sauce featuring broccoli, and sometimes baked ricotta, crushed anchovy fillets, chopped chard, cavolo nero, spinach, rocket, fava beans and peas (see page 72).

When cooking pasta keep in mind that salting the water not only helps cooking but also seasons the pasta. (It is impossible to season pasta later, and unseasoned pasta is bland and uninteresting.) Don't bother to add oil to the pan, as this is quite unnecessary. When the pasta is al dente, drain it only briefly so that it still retains moisture, then add it to your pan of sauce, toss it through and let it cook for a minute or so more to amalgamate the flavours. This is far more effective than ladling sauce on top of pasta and having people attempt to toss the sauce themselves within their own plate or bowl.

**buffalo ricotta** Ricotta isn't really a cheese, it is made from re-cooking the whey that is separated out during cheesemaking. More expensive than cow's-milk ricotta, buffalo ricotta from Naples is darker and more flavoursome. Use it with good spinach, seasoned with nutmeg, as a filling for home-made ravioli, and you will understand why this combination, so often made bland by indifferent ingredients, was created.

**gnocchi** Gnocchi means dumplings, and there are two main types of gnocchi: semolina-based and potato-based. At Daphne's only potato gnocchi are made, as they are the most versatile. The potatoes to use are red-skinned waxy ones, and the secret is to handle the dough very lightly. However, making really good gnocchi is something that will come only with patience and practice (see page 86).

**pesto** The famous sauce that can be run through pasta or drizzled over grilled vegetables is only as good as its ingredients. Quality is everything. Everyone has their own opinion as to exactly what those ingredients should be. The fundamentals are basil, oil and garlic, then you could add parsley, pine nuts or walnuts, or a mixture of both nuts. Some people even put in almonds. Walnuts tends to make the pesto more bitter than pine nuts, so if adding them, it is probably best to use a mixture, rather than solely walnuts. The other debate is whether to add Pecorino or Parmesan — it is up to you. A southern Italian variant of pesto is the chunky anchovy & olive salsa (see page 27).

# basic pasta dough

MAKES 1 KILO/2LB

1kg/2lb 00 *flour*

6 eggs, *beaten*

50ml/2fl oz *extra virgin olive oil*

50g/2oz *salt*

1   On a flat surface, heap the flour and use your hands to make a well in the centre.

2   Add the eggs, olive oil and salt to the well. With your hands, carefully start to push the flour into the well, working it into the egg mixture. Keep kneading until you have a smooth ball of dough.

3   If not using immediately, cover the dough with plastic wrap and refrigerate until needed. The dough will keep for up to 3 or 4 days in the refrigerator.

# pappardelle with rabbit

1 rabbit, *meat separated and roughly diced, bones reserved (your butcher can do this for you)*

400g/13oz *pappardelle*

*salt and freshly ground black pepper*

**for the marinade**

125g/4oz *carrots, roughly diced*

125g/4oz *leeks, outer leaves removed, thoroughly washed and roughly diced*

125g/4oz *celery, roughly diced*

125g/4oz *onions, roughly diced*

25g/1oz *fresh oregano leaves*

½ *garlic bulb, cut in half*

10 *black peppercorns*

300ml/½ pint *white wine*

**for the sauce**

*rabbit bones, reserved from rabbit above*

50ml/2fl oz *vegetable oil*

125g/4oz *carrots, roughly diced*

125g/4oz *leeks, outer leaves removed, thoroughly washed and roughly diced*

125g/4oz *celery, roughly diced*

125g/4oz *onions, roughly diced*

4 *garlic cloves, crushed*

1 *thyme or rosemary sprig*

200ml/7fl oz *tomato passata* (see page 33)

2 litres/3½ pints *chicken stock* (see page 21)

25g/1oz *fresh oregano leaves, finely chopped*

75g/3oz *black olives, pitted and finely chopped*

**for the garnish**

25g/1oz *Pecorino, shaved*

1   Overnight, marinate the rabbit meat with the vegetables, oregano, garlic, peppercorns and white wine. Drain the wine and reserve.

2   To make the sauce, chop the rabbit bones into very small pieces. Heat a large heavy-based pan (the larger the base the better) over high heat and add a third of the vegetable oil. Seal the rabbit meat in the pan, about 4–5 minutes, then remove and reserve. Add half the remaining vegetable oil and when smoking add the bones. Cook in the pan over high heat, stirring occasionally, until the bones are browned, about 10–12 minutes. Remove bones and reserve.

3   Add the remaining vegetable oil with the carrots, leeks, celery, onions, garlic and thyme or rosemary and cook over high heat, stirring occasionally until golden brown, about 7–8 minutes. Add the tomato passata and cook to reduce by four-fifths, about 4 minutes. Then add the wine reserved from the marinade and reduced by four-fifths, about 3 minutes. Add the chicken stock and bring to the boil. Add the rabbit bones and gently simmer for an hour to reduce, skimming regularly to remove any impurities. Remove bones from pan. Remove garlic and rosemary and discard.

4   Place the meat in the stock and simmer for 40 minutes. Season to taste and keep warm.

5   Boil a large pan of salted water and cook the pappardelle until al dente, about 7–8 minutes, and drain. Add the oregano, black olives and pappardelle to the sauce and cook together on a medium heat for 1 minute.

6   Divide between serving plates and garnish with shaved Pecorino.

• *Serve with Chianti Classico.*

 *If the sauce seems too thin once you have finished cooking the rabbit meat, remove the meat from the sauce and boil until it has reduced to the desired consistency. Then add the meat back in and continue. Although pappardelle and rabbit traditionally make perfect partners, if you prefer to use duck or guinea fowl, they will work equally well.*

SPAGHETTI SEAFOOD
(RECIPE FOLLOWS)

# spaghetti seafood

100ml/3½fl oz *extra virgin olive oil*

4 large *langoustines*

200g/7oz *squid, cleaned and ink sacs removed, half the body sliced into rings, half diced, tentacles left whole*

200g/7oz *clams (or cockles), washed well*

125g/4oz *raw or pre-cooked Tiger prawns*

200g/7oz *mussels, beards removed, and washed well*

1 *chilli, deseeded and finely chopped*

1 *garlic clove, crushed*

200ml/7fl oz *white wine*

200g/7oz *tomatoes, roughly diced*

1 litre/1¼ pints *fish stock (see page 20)*

400g/13oz *spaghettini*

*salt and freshly ground black pepper*

**for the garnish**

50g/2oz *flat-leaf parsley, finely shredded*

1  Heat a large heavy-based saucepan over a low heat and add the olive oil. When smoking, add the langoustines, squid, clams, prawns, mussels, chilli and garlic. Cover with a lid and cook gently for 2 minutes. (If using pre-cooked prawns, add these for the last 30 seconds.)

2  Add the white wine and reduce until the alcohol has burnt out (the alcohol will no longer have a 'kick' to it when you smell it).

3  Remove the seafood from the pan with a slotted spoon, discarding mussels and clams that have not opened, then add the tomatoes and fish stock. Season lightly to taste.

4  Bring to the boil and reduce by half. Turn off the heat and return the seafood to the saucepan. Leave to stand while you cook the pasta.

5  Boil some salted water in a large saucepan and cook the pasta for 6–7 minutes until al dente. Drain the pasta and stir it into the sauce. Cook for a further minute, then check the seasoning.

6  Sprinkle with parsley and serve immediately.

• *Serve with Verdicchio.*

*Make sure that the mussels and clams are cleaned meticulously (see page 111) as one gritty one could ruin the delicate flavours and textures of this dish.*

# salt cod & potato ravioli with clams & parsley

*00 flour for rolling out*

125g/4oz *pasta dough* (see page 66)

**for the filling**

200g/7oz *cod baccala* (see page 139)

**for the sauce**

125g/4oz *clams, washed well*

100ml/3½fl oz *white wine*

200g/7oz *unsalted butter, chilled*

50g/2oz *flat-leaf parsley, finely shredded*

juice of 1 *lemon*

*salt and freshly ground black pepper*

1  On a floured surface, roll the pasta dough out to about 3mm/⅛in thick.

2  Cut the dough into squares with a knife or use a ravioli press or pasta wheel for this.

3  Place a portion of cod baccala mix in the centre of half the pasta squares, brush the edges with water, then place the remaining squares on top to make ravioli parcels. Seal the edges carefully with your fingertips (avoid leaving bubbles in the centre of the squares).

4  Cover the ravioli with a damp cloth to prevent them from drying out and set aside.

5  Heat through a heavy-based saucepan and when hot add the clams and cover with a lid for just 30 seconds.

6  Add the white wine and cover again. Leave to reduce (all the clams should be open), about 4 minutes. Transfer the clams to a plate using a slotted spoon. Discard any that have not opened.

7  Return the saucepan to a low heat and gradually whisk in the butter. Add the parsley, lemon juice and clams. Season and keep the sauce warm.

8  Bring a large saucepan full of salted water to the boil and cook the ravioli for 1 minute until al dente. Drain the pasta and stir it into the sauce. Cook the two together gently for 1 minute, then serve.

• *Serve with Chablis.*

# orecchiette with baked ricotta, wild greens & truffle oil

300g/10oz *ricotta cheese*

400g/13oz *orecchiette*

50g/2oz *pine nuts, toasted* (see page 13)

*salt and freshly ground black pepper*

**for the sauce**

500ml/17fl oz *extra virgin olive oil*

125g/4oz *onion, roughly diced*

50g/2oz *anchovy fillets, crushed*

2 *garlic cloves, crushed with salt to a purée*

1 *chilli, deseeded and chopped*

1 *rosemary sprig, leaves picked and finely chopped*

1 *thyme sprig, leaves picked and finely chopped*

125g/4oz *green cauliflower heads, quartered*

125g/4oz *cime di rapa or young turnip tops, leaves removed and roughly chopped*

125g/4oz *Swiss chard, leaves removed and roughly chopped*

125g/4oz *cavolo nero or Savoy cabbage, leaves removed and roughly chopped*

200g/7oz *spinach, freshly picked (if possible) and chopped*

125g/4oz *rocket, chopped*

50g/2oz *fava (broad) beans, peeled*

50g/2oz *fresh garden peas*

**for the garnish**

*white truffle oil, to taste*

1 Preheat oven to 120°C (250°F), Gas Mark ½. Cover a baking sheet with baking paper. Place the ricotta on top and bake, uncovered, for 1 hour until firm to the touch. Leave to cool on the baking tray while you prepare the sauce.

2 Warm a large heavy-based saucepan, then add the olive oil and heat through slowly. When hot, add the onion, anchovies, garlic purée, chilli, rosemary and thyme. Sauté for 5 minutes.

3 Add the green cauliflower and sauté for a further 5 minutes. Then add the cime di rapa, Swiss chard, cavolo nero, spinach and rocket and sauté for 5 minutes.

4 Add the fava beans and peas to the saucepan and sauté for a further 5 minutes. Season and leave the sauce to cool in the saucepan.

5 Meanwhile, boil some salted water in a large saucepan and cook the pasta for about 6–7 minutes until al dente.

6 Drain the pasta and toss it together with the sauce. Flake the baked ricotta and add it to the mixture, together with the pine nuts. Check the seasoning.

7 Place some of the tossed pasta in the centre of each plate and drizzle white truffle oil around the edge.

• *Serve with Chardonnay.*

# tagliolini with white truffle

| |
|---|
| 400g/13oz *tagliolini* |
| 20g/¼oz *butter, plus extra for thickening sauce* |
| 125g/4oz *shallots, roughly diced* |
| 400ml/14fl oz *chicken stock* (see page 21) |
| 20g/¼oz *white truffle (from Alba if possible)* |
| *salt and freshly ground black pepper* |

1 In a large saucepan full of boiling, salted water, cook the tagliolini for 8–10 minutes, depending on the quality of the pasta, until al dente.

2 Meanwhile, in a large frying pan, melt the butter and sauté the shallots until they are cooked but not coloured, about 7–8 minutes.

3 Add the chicken stock, gently boil to reduce the liquid by half and add a knob of butter to thicken it if necessary. Then add the cooked tagliolini. Toss the mixture together and heat through gently. Check the seasoning.

4 Serve on individual, heated plates and, at the table, slice the truffle very thinly over the top of each dish to appreciate the truffle's full aroma.

• *Serve with a wood-aged Chardonnay.*

 *Always shave truffles as finely as possible. Store them in the fridge next to your eggs or rice — to make truffle-scented scrambled eggs or risotto.*

# scallop &
# rosemary ravioli

125g/4oz *pasta dough* (see page 66)

*salt and freshly ground black pepper*

**for the scallop mousse filling**

4 large *scallops*

100ml/3½fl oz *white wine*

50g/2oz *rosemary, leaves picked and finely chopped*

1 *egg white, beaten*

200ml/7fl oz *double cream*

**for the sauce**

125g/4oz *butter*

50g/2oz *capers*

80g/3¼oz *plum tomatoes, skins removed, deseeded and chopped*

80g/3¼oz *fava (broad) beans, peeled and blanched*

80g/3¼oz *haricots verts, blanched and cut to the same size as the beans*

**for the garnish**

20g/¼oz *flat-leaf parsley, finely shredded*

1  To make the scallop mousse filling, place the scallops in a large heavy-based saucepan and just cover with water. Bring to the boil, turn off heat and leave the scallops to cool in the liquid. Clean the scallops, removing the excess beards, and slice and reserve the roe for the sauce.

2  In the bowl of a food processor fitted with the metal blade, place the white scallop meat. Add the white wine and rosemary and whiz for 1 minute. Add the egg white and whiz for 20 seconds to bind the mixture. Pass the mixture through a fine sieve into a large bowl. Leave to cool, covered, in the refrigerator for 10 minutes.

3  Gradually add the cream to the mixture, a quarter at a time, and mix it in well. Return the mousse to the refrigerator for 10 minutes in between each addition of cream.

4  For this recipe, do a little test to check the seasoning. In a small saucepan, boil some water then add a spoonful of the mousse. Cook for 20 seconds, remove from the saucepan and taste. Correct the seasoning as necessary.

5  Roll the pasta dough through a pasta machine on the thinnest setting to make 2 sheets. On the first sheet, place small teaspoons of scallop mix, evenly spaced about 10cm/4in apart. Brush a little water around each dollop of mix and lay the second sheet on top. Using a serrated cutter, cut the sheets into individual ravioli and seal the edges of each with damp fingertips.

6  To make the sauce, place a large heavy-based saucepan over a low heat until hot, then add the butter. When it begins to foam and brown, about 1 minute, add the capers, tomatoes, fava beans, haricots verts and sliced scallop roe. Sauté for 1 minute and keep warm while cooking the pasta.

7  Bring a large saucepan of salted water to the boil, add the ravioli and simmer for 2 minutes until al dente. Drain and add to the sauce.

8  Add the flat-leaf parsley to the ravioli and check the seasoning again before serving.

• *Serve with Sauvignon Blanc.*

# porcini & artichoke ravioli

| |
|---|
| 1 *lemon, cut in half* |
| 2 *artichokes, peeled, hearts and excess leaves removed, and rubbed with lemon (above)* |
| 50ml/2fl oz *extra virgin olive oil* |
| 50g/2oz *butter* |
| 200g/7oz *fresh porcini, sliced (set aside 50g/2oz of these for the sauce)* |
| 50g/2oz *onion, finely diced* |
| 50g/2oz *pancetta, finely diced* |
| 50g/2oz *flat-leaf parsley, finely shredded* |
| 00 *flour for rolling out* |
| 125g/4oz *pasta dough (see page 66)* |
| 1 litre/1¼ pints *chicken stock (see page 21)* |
| *salt and freshly ground black pepper* |

1 To make the ravioli filling, place the artichokes in a saucepan and cover with water. Add salt and cook until soft, about 15 minutes. Drain and cut into fine dice. Place in a large bowl and set aside.

2 Heat the olive oil and butter in a deep frying pan. Add the porcini and onion. Sauté until golden brown, about 6 minutes. Season well and leave to cool. Reserve the olive oil/butter.

3 Dice the porcini into 5mm/¼in pieces and add them to the artichokes, together with the pancetta and parsley. Mix the ingredients together and check the seasoning.

4 On a floured surface, roll the pasta dough out to a sheet 2mm/¹⁄₁₆in thick and use a knife, ravioli press or pasta wheel to cut it into ravioli squares.

5 Place a teaspoon of filling in the centre of half the squares. Brush the edges of all the squares with water, then place one of the remaining squares on top of each filled one. Seal the edges together with your fingers, making sure there are no bubbles in the centre of the squares.

6 Cover the ravioli with a damp cloth to prevent them from drying out and set aside.

7 To make the sauce, reheat the olive oil/butter in the frying pan and sauté the remaining porcini. Add the chicken stock and reduce by three-quarters. Keep warm.

8 Fill a large saucepan with water. Add salt and bring to the boil. Then add the prepared ravioli and simmer for 3 minutes until al dente. Drain, add to the prepared sauce and serve.

• *Serve with Chardonnay.*

 *The ravioli can be made in advance and stored in the refrigerator for 2 days if blanched for a minute first. When ready to use, cook the ravioli for 3 minutes.*

# garganelli with Parma ham, rocket, radicchio & pine nuts

400g/13oz *garganelli*

125g/4oz *coppa di Parma, very thinly sliced*

50g/2oz *rocket, very thinly sliced*

50g/2oz *radicchio, stalk removed, very thinly sliced*

50g/2oz *pine nuts, toasted* (see page 13)

50g/2oz *flat-leaf parsley, finely shredded*

200ml/7fl oz *shallot oil* (see penne with courgettes, walnuts & Pecorino, page 85)

50g/2oz *freshly grated Parmesan*

*salt and freshly ground black pepper*

1  Fill a saucepan with salted water, bring to the boil, then add the pasta. Cook for 6–7 minutes until al dente and drain.
2  In a large bowl, toss all the ingredients apart from the pasta gently together.
3  Add the pasta, then check the seasoning and serve immediately.

• *Serve with Pinot Grigio.*

# penne with peppers, aubergine & mozzarella

2 *aubergines, cut into 2.5cm/1in circles*

100ml/3½fl oz *extra virgin olive oil, plus extra for drizzling*

3 *peppers (mixed colours)*

1 *thyme sprig*

500g/1lb *penne*

6 *cherry tomatoes (as ripe as possible), finely chopped*

6 *plum tomatoes (as ripe as possible), finely chopped*

2 *garlic cloves, crushed*

1 *chilli, deseeded and chopped*

10 *basil leaves, torn (reserve half for the garnish)*

*salt and freshly ground black pepper*

**for the garnish**

250g/8oz *buffalo mozzarella, diced*

This dish is best if you cook the vegetables a day before and marinate them in advance.

1  Brush the aubergines with olive oil and chargrill, or grill, on both sides until soft. Season well and cut into pieces that are about the same size as the pasta.

2  Roast the peppers evenly over a chargrill, or under a grill, then peel and deseed them. Cut into pieces the same size as the pasta. Leave to cool, then season well and store in an airtight container with a little olive oil and thyme.

3  Bring a saucepan full of salted water to the boil. Add the penne, reduce the heat and simmer for about 4 minutes, until almost al dente (cooking time depends on pasta quality).

4  Meanwhile, warm a frying pan and when hot add some olive oil and the tomatoes. Sauté the tomatoes with the garlic and chilli until the mixture starts to break down.

5  Add the aubergines and peppers to the frying pan. Toss the mixture together and when the penne is just al dente drain and add it to the pan. Leave the pasta to finish cooking in the sauce, about 1–2 minutes. Season and finish with half the torn basil leaves.

6  To make the garnish, in a bowl mix the mozzarella with the remaining torn basil. Add some olive oil to bind the mixture together and season well.

7  Divide the pasta among 4 serving plates. Place some of the garnish on top of each pile of pasta and drizzle over a little olive oil.

• *Serve with Chianti Classico.*

# linguini clams

800g/1lb 10oz *linguini*

100ml/3½fl oz *extra virgin olive oil*

400g/13oz *clams, washed well*

100ml/3½fl oz *white wine*

50g/2oz *butter*

50g/2oz *shallots, finely diced*

150g/4oz *cherry tomatoes, halved*

1 *garlic clove, crushed*

½ *chilli, deseeded and finely chopped*

100ml/3½fl oz *vegetable stock* (see page 20)

4 tbsps *anchovy and olive salsa* (see page 27)

handful *finely chopped flat-leaf parsley*

*salt and freshly ground black pepper*

1  Bring a large saucepan of salted water to the boil and cook the linguini until almost al dente, about 7–8 minutes. Drain and keep warm.

2  Meanwhile, warm a large heavy-based saucepan over a low heat so that it is nice and hot. Pour in the oil and when it is almost smoking, about 3 minutes, add the clams and cover with a lid. After 1 minute, add the white wine and cook until the alcohol has been reduced by half, about 2–3 minutes.

3  Remove the saucepan from the heat and transfer the contents to a heatproof bowl. Cover with plastic wrap so that it is airtight.

4  Return the saucepan to a low heat. Melt a knob of butter in it and add the shallots, tomatoes, garlic and chilli. Cook, tossing the mixture occasionally, until the shallots are soft, about 4 minutes. Add the vegetable stock to the saucepan and slowly bring to the boil.

5  Return the clam mixture to the saucepan and bring back to the boil. Add the pasta and anchovy and olive salsa to the clam sauce. (Use more or less salsa, according to taste.) Simmer for about 1 minute to allow the pasta to completely absorb the flavour of the clams.

6  Add some parsley to the pasta and season. If you prefer a richer sauce, you can add more butter before serving.

• *Serve with Corvo Bianco.*

# salmon, spinach, rocket & ricotta rotolo

*00 flour for rolling out*

*200g/7oz pasta dough* (see page 66)

*1 egg yolk*

*300g/10oz fresh salmon fillet, pinboned, skinned and thinly sliced (your fishmonger can do this for you)*

*salt and freshly ground black pepper*

**for the filling**

*20g/¾oz butter*

*50g/2oz onion, finely diced*

*2 garlic cloves, crushed with salt to a purée*

*125g/4oz spinach, freshly picked (if possible) and roughly chopped*

*300g/10oz buffalo ricotta*

*freshly grated nutmeg, to taste*

*1 egg yolk*

**for the garnish**

*125g/4oz rocket*

*extra virgin olive oil for drizzling*

*50g/2oz Parmesan, shaved*

1. For the filling, melt the butter in a saucepan over low heat, then add the onion and puréed garlic cloves and cook without allowing them to colour, about 6–7 minutes.

2. Add the spinach to the mixture and cook for about 5 minutes until wilted. Season and set aside to cool.

3. In a large bowl, mix together the buffalo ricotta, nutmeg and egg yolk and season well.

4. On a floured surface, roll the pasta out to a sheet measuring about 30 x 30cm/12 x 12in and 3mm/⅛in thick.

5. Brush the sheet with egg yolk, then place the salmon slices on top so that they overlap without any gaps, leaving a border of about 2½cm/1in around the edges. Season to taste.

6. Spread a thin layer of the spinach mixture on top of the salmon, then add a layer of ricotta (use about two-thirds of the mixture).

7. Place the remaining ricotta at the base of the pasta sheet. Brush the edges of the sheet with water to help seal them, then roll the pasta up into a cylinder.

8. Wrap the pasta roll in plastic wrap and cook it in a bain-marie (or deep tray filled with boiling water) for 20 minutes.

9. Meanwhile, in a bowl toss the rocket with olive oil and Parmesan. When the pasta is cooked, drain and serve it on a plate, garnished with the rocket mixture.

• *Serve with Franciacorta.*

# anolini nero with sea bass, saffron & tomato

dash of *white wine*

large pinch *saffron threads*

125g/4oz *pasta dough* (see page 66), *rolled up into 2 separate balls*

*00 flour for rolling out*

*squid ink (from your fishmonger), just enough to colour the pasta black*

salt and freshly ground black pepper

*for the filling*

500g/1lb *sea bass, gutted (your fishmonger can do this for you)*

50ml/2fl oz *extra virgin olive oil, plus extra for drizzling*

50g/2oz *chives, finely chopped*

50g/2oz *flat-leaf parsley, finely chopped*

*lemon juice, to taste*

*for the sauce*

125g/4oz *butter*

50g/2oz *tomatoes, skins removed, deseeded and roughly diced*

100ml/3½fl oz *fish stock* (see page 20)

80g/3¼oz *samphire, freshly picked and blanched*

*lemon juice, to taste*

1　Preheat oven to 180°C (350°F), Gas Mark 4.

2　To make the filling, place the sea bass drizzled with oil in a roasting tin and roast it whole for 12–15 minutes until just cooked.

3　Remove the meat from the fish and take out any tiny bones that remain.

4　In a large bowl, mix the fish with the chives, parsley, olive oil and lemon juice. Season well and set aside.

5　To make the anolini, warm the white wine in a small saucepan. Add the saffron and leave to infuse, about 20 minutes, to bring out the taste and colour of the spice. Leave to cool.

6　In a bowl, mix the white wine with half the pasta dough. Mix the remaining dough with the squid ink (enough to colour the pasta black).

7　With the pasta machine set at 3–4, put the two lots of pasta through the machine separately to make two sheets measuring about 12cm/5in square and 5mm/¼in thick. On a floured surface, cut the pasta sheets into strips, about 4cm/1½in wide.

8　Overlap alternate strips of pasta colours, brushing water on the overlapping areas to seal, to create one striped sheet. Then roll through the pasta machine at 1–2 thickness.

9　Cut the pasta sheet into circles about 8cm/3in in diameter and place a small amount of sea bass filling inside (enough to be able to fold the circles in half without splitting). Brush the edges with water and then fold and seal carefully to make semi-circular anolini.

10　To make the sauce, warm a large heavy-based saucepan and add a knob of butter. Sauté the tomatoes, about 5 minutes, and add the fish stock. Reduce by half, then whisk in the remaining butter. Add the samphire, check the seasoning and add a dash of lemon juice.

11　Bring a large heavy-based saucepan of salted water to the boil. Add the anolini and simmer for 1 minute until al dente. Drain and add the pasta to the sauce. Cook for 1 minute.

12　Pour a little sauce in the centre of each plate and place the anolini in sauce on top.

• *Serve with Chardonnay or Sauvignon Blanc.*

# lobster &
# fennel ravioli

*for the lobster sauce*

| |
|---|
| 1 *live lobster, weighing about 500g/1lb* |
| 1 tbsp *olive oil* |
| ½ *garlic clove, finely chopped* |
| 1 *shallot, finely chopped* |
| 1 *celery stick, finely chopped* |
| 2 tbsps *Pernod* |
| 50g/2oz *butter, chilled* |
| 2 *tomatoes, skins removed, deseeded and roughly diced* |
| *salt and freshly ground black pepper* |

*for the ravioli*

| |
|---|
| 1 head of *fennel, green shoots and coarse outer leaves removed* |
| 600ml/1 pint *milk* |
| 1 *bay leaf* |
| 200g/7oz *ricotta cheese* |
| 250g/8oz *pasta dough (see page 66)* |
| 00 *flour for rolling out* |

*for the garnish*

| |
|---|
| ½ bunch *dill, chopped* |

1 Plunge the lobster into a large saucepan of boiling salted water for 2 minutes in order to kill it and free the meat from the shell (or your fishmonger can do this for you). Remove and transfer to a large bowl of cold water.

2 Crack the lobster claws with the blunt handle of a heavy knife and cut the tail in half. Remove all the meat from the shells and roughly chop it, reserving the shells.

3 Place the shells inside a large heavy-based saucepan and crush with a rolling pin. Pour over enough water to cover them and simmer gently for 30 minutes.

4 Pass the stock created from the shells through a fine sieve into a smaller saucepan and reduce down to about 250ml/8fl oz, then set aside.

5 Meanwhile, to make the ravioli, cut the fennel in half lengthways and remove and discard the core. Roughly chop the fennel and place in a saucepan with the milk and the bay leaf. Simmer gently for approximately 30 minutes, or until very tender, to remove any bitterness from the fennel. Drain and leave to cool.

6 In the bowl of a food processor fitted with the metal blade, purée the fennel. Mix in the ricotta, then season well and pass through a fine sieve into a bowl. Cover with plastic wrap and refrigerate until needed.

7 On a floured surface, roll out the pasta dough into the thinnest sheet possible. Use a knife, ravioli press or pasta wheel to cut it into 32 squares, each measuring about 6cm/2½in.

8 Place a teaspoon of filling into the centre of half the squares and brush the edges of all the squares with water. Place the remaining squares on top and seal each one firmly with your fingertips, making sure that there are no bubbles in the centre. Cover with a damp cloth and set aside.

9 Heat the tablespoon of olive oil in a pan and add the garlic, shallots and celery. Cook for 3 minutes, then flame with Pernod. Pour in the

# penne with courgettes, walnuts & Pecorino

400g/13oz *courgettes, marinated in anchovy oil*

2 *mint leaves, chopped*

400g/13oz *penne*

125g/4oz *fresh walnuts, shelled and peeled*

125g/4oz *Pecorino, cut into chunks*

50g/2oz *flat-leaf parsley, freshly picked (if possible), chopped*

100ml/3½fl oz *shallot oil* (see method)

*salt and freshly ground black pepper*

**for the shallot oil**

200g/7oz *shallots*

10 *black peppercorns*

1 *chilli, deseeded and finely chopped*

1 litre/1¼ pints *olive oil*

For this recipe, the shallot oil needs to be started at least 4–6 hours in advance.

1  Mix all the shallot oil ingredients in a saucepan. Heat gently and then leave, covered, to infuse for 4–6 hours. This can be stored in a sealed container in a cool, dark place for 2–3 weeks.

2  Chargrill (or lightly fry in olive oil) the courgettes until half-cooked, about 2–3 minutes, and cut into pieces the same size as the penne. Add the mint and leave to infuse for an hour.

3  Bring a large saucepan of salted water to the boil and cook the penne for about 8–10 minutes (depending on the pasta quality) until al dente.

4  Drain the pasta and place it in a large bowl. Add the courgettes, walnuts, Pecorino, parsley and shallot oil. Toss all the ingredients together and season to taste.

• *Serve with Chardonnay.*

---

lobster stock and bring to the boil.

10  Remove the sauce from the heat and whisk in the chilled butter. Add the tomatoes and lobster meat. Heat through gently and season to taste. Keep warm.

11  Bring a large saucepan of salted water to the boil and cook the ravioli until al dente, about 3 minutes. Drain and place 4 ravioli on each plate. Spoon over sauce and garnish with dill.

• *Serve with Sauvignon Blanc.*

# gnocchi

500g/1lb *red potatoes, Desiree redskin or Irish redskin*

50g/2oz *freshly grated Parmesan*

pinch *grated nutmeg*

1 *egg*

125g/4oz *00 flour, plus extra for rolling out*

125g/4oz *plain flour*

*(semolina or maize can be substituted)*

*salt and freshly ground black pepper*

 *The only way to make gnocchi is by hand and homemade is far better than the commercial variety. This recipe can be made in advance: blanch the gnocchi for 1 minute in boiling, salted water and then store in oil in kilner jars for up to 2 days, or freeze on trays for up to 7 days until needed. Gnocchi are particularly good served with a fresh pumpkin sauce (see recipe on page 89).*

1  Boil the potatoes in their skins until tender (about 35–40 minutes). Remove from the heat and drain through a colander or sieve.

2  Peel the skins from the hot potatoes and pass through a sieve into a large bowl.

3  Stir in seasoning, Parmesan and nutmeg.

4  Whisk the egg in a separate bowl, then make a well in the potato mixture. Add the whisked egg and gradually incorporate the mixture together with your hands.

5  Sieve both flours into the bowl and mix the ingredients together gently until they are incorporated. Remove the potato mixture from the bowl and, as gently as possible, knead it for about 3 minutes to form a dough.

6  Depending on the moistness of the potatoes, the flour content for this recipe may vary. The dough should be smooth and soft. If it feels sticky, add a little more flour.

7  On a floured surface, roll out the dough and cut it into long strips. Cut the strips into batons measuring about 2.5–5cm/1–2in long. Gently, but firmly enough to produce a ribbed effect, press the back of a fork into the back of each baton. (The ribbed effect will allow whatever sauce you choose to serve with the gnocchi to stick to it.)

# pumpkin gnocchi

1 *pumpkin*

1 bunch *sage, leaves picked and stalk reserved*

4 *garlic cloves, crushed*

400ml/14fl oz *vegetable stock* (see page 20)

100ml/3½fl oz *olive oil*

125g/4oz *speck, cut into pieces the same size as the gnocchi*

500g/1lb *plain gnocchi* (see page 86)

50g/2oz *freshly grated Parmesan*

*salt and freshly ground black pepper*

1 Preheat oven to 180°C (350°F), Gas Mark 2. Cut the pumpkin in half and remove seeds.

2 Score the inside of the pumpkin with a knife, careful not to pierce the skin, sprinkle with salt and pepper, sage stalks and garlic and roast on a tray in the oven for about 30–40 minutes (until the pumpkin is cooked and can be scraped from the skin). Leave for 10 minutes.

3 Using a spoon, scrape all the pumpkin from the shell, then put into a food processor and whiz to a fine purée. Blend in the stock and check seasoning.

4 Heat the olive oil in a large saucepan and gently fry the speck for 2 minutes. Add the sage leaves and cook for a further minute, then add the pumpkin sauce. Bring to the boil, then reduce to lowest heat and check seasoning.

5 Meanwhile, cook the gnocchi in boiling salted water for a minute, then drain and add to the pumpkin sauce. Gently fold together and remove from heat.

6 Serve in shallow bowls and sprinkle with Parmesan.

• *Serve with Soave Classico.*

# grains & pulses

risotto base

risotto with courgette flowers

wild mushroom risotto

porcini risotto

risotto with asparagus

risotto primavera

risotto with seafood & saffron

squab & wild mushroom risotto

polenta

braised Umbrian lentils

minestrone & farro soup

lentil soup

 IN RECENT YEARS THE ROLE OF STORE-CUPBOARD STAPLES LIKE RICE, BEANS AND LENTILS HAS BEEN TRANSFORMED. RISOTTOS HAVE TAKEN ON A NEW ELEGANCE, WHILE LENTILS, CHICKPEAS AND BEANS, ONCE USED JUST TO ADD BULK, ARE NOW SEEN AS EXCITING INGREDIENTS IN THEIR OWN RIGHT.

# arborio rice
Risotto rice has a high starch content, which allows it to thicken and stick together in a way that long grain doesn't, yet still retain a bite in the middle, unlike Asian sticky rice. There are three types of risotto rice: arborio, vialone and carnaroli, each of which has its ardent supporters. Arborio is the easiest to find outside Italy and is the one favoured at Daphne's because it is the most consistent, producing creamy, evenly cooked grains.

# cannellini beans
Creamy white cannellini beans can be used fresh or dried. It is worth paying a little more to buy the biggest, which are best cooked in the simple traditional manner with a prosciutto hock, garlic and vegetables, covered with stock and herbs (see page 23). If using dried beans, soak them overnight in five times their volume of water to allow them room to swell up properly. Never salt the water at the beginning of cooking, because a chemical reaction makes the skins toughen. When they are soft (about 2 hours), pull the pan off the heat and salt the water quite generously so the beans can absorb the seasoning while warm, then, if you like, add some extra virgin olive oil.

# white polenta
Made around Venice, using only the inside of the corn, not the husk, white polenta is seen as something quite luxurious; yellow polenta is considered more of a peasant dish. This is the polenta to convert people who think that cornmeal porridge has no flavour or appeal. It is delicate, creamy and smooth-textured, a perfect partner for dishes like liver Veneziana (see page 155). Cook it in a mixture of half milk, half water, with some garlic purée and bay leaves, so that the milk can maintain the white colour and make the polenta even creamier.

**borlotti beans** When fresh, from about September to mid-January, borlotti beans are speckled red and white, and turn pink as soon as they begin to cook. They are similar to cannellini beans, but rougher in texture and more starchy. The texture analogy used in the Daphne's kitchen is that cannellini are the equivalent of new potatoes, so could be used, for example, in light fish dishes; borlotti are more like baked potatoes, and are good in dishes like chunky mussel soups (see page 127).

**farro** Known as spelt in Britain, this is an ancient variety of wheat used in Roman times. It is used like a small pasta, in soups like a rustic minestrone made with pancetta and ciabatta (see page 107).

**chickpeas** In Italian cooking chickpeas are used chiefly in soup. They are cooked in a similar way to cannellini and borlotti beans, but because they have a tendency to harden slightly after cooking, when they appear to be ready, i.e. just soft, give them a little longer before taking off the heat. Chickpeas need a good deal of salt because of their density. Like beans, they should be salted at the end of cooking time, rather than the beginning, or the skins will toughen.

**Umbrian lentils** Grown around Assisi, these very expensive lentils are even smaller than Puy lentils and need to be cooked very gently to keep them intact. Whereas Puy lentils are more suited to soup, the delicate nature of the Umbrian lentil lends itself to being served with fish, either braised (see page 104) or in a warm salad (see page 140).

# risotto base

MAKES 600G/1 ¼LB

50ml/2fl oz *extra virgin olive oil*

1 medium *onion, finely chopped*

1 *garlic clove, crushed with salt to a purée*

200g/7oz *risotto rice*

1 litre/1 ¾ pints *vegetable stock* (see page 20)

1  Heat the olive oil in a large heavy-based
   saucepan and add the onion and garlic.
   Cook slowly, shaking the saucepan occasionally,
   for about 5 minutes until the onions and garlic
   are transparent.

2  Add the rice and continue to cook for
   2 minutes, stirring all the time.

3  Add the vegetable stock gradually and cook
   slowly, stirring constantly, until the liquid has
   been absorbed by the rice, about 15 minutes.

 *The risotto base above is cooked three-quarters of
the way through, ready to be used in risotto dishes,
or to be cooked as is for a further 5 minutes, grated
Parmesan, butter and seasoning stirred in, and served simply with
shavings of white truffle on top. The risotto base can be made in
advance and stored in the refrigerator for up to 3 days.*

# risotto with courgette flowers

| |
|---|
| 200g/7oz *courgettes with flowers* |
| *extra virgin olive oil for frying* |
| 2 *mint leaves, finely chopped* |
| 600g/1¼lb *risotto base* (see page 94) |
| 450ml/¾ pint *vegetable stock* (see page 20) |
| 200g/7oz *butter* |
| 125g/4oz *freshly grated Parmesan* |
| *salt and freshly ground black pepper* |

1  Separate the flowers from the courgettes and reserve them for the garnish. Slice the courgettes thinly.

2  Warm a tablespoon of olive oil in a large heavy-based frying pan and add the courgettes and mint. Sauté for 2 minutes, then add the rice base and mix together thoroughly.

3  Add the stock, stirring in a little at a time, until almost all the liquid has been absorbed and the rice is cooked, about 5 minutes.

4  Continue stirring the risotto and add the butter and Parmesan to form a rich and creamy texture when they are melted.

5  Season to taste and serve, garnished with the reserved courgette flowers.

• *Serve with Bianco di Custoza.*

# wild mushroom risotto

---

garlic oil for frying (see page 10)

375g/12oz mixed fresh wild mushrooms such as porcini, chanterelles, trompettes, pied de mouton

1 rosemary sprig, chopped

600g/1¼lb risotto base (see page 94)

450ml/¾ pint vegetable stock (see page 20)

125g/4oz butter

125g/4oz freshly grated Parmesan

salt and freshly ground black pepper

---

1   Heat some garlic oil in a large heavy-based frying pan and sauté the mushrooms with a little rosemary, shaking the pan occasionally, for 2–3 minutes. Season well.

2   Add the risotto base and the vegetable stock. Continue to cook, stirring, for a further 4–5 minutes until all the liquid has been absorbed and the rice is cooked.

3   Remove the frying pan from the heat and carefully stir in the butter and Parmesan to form a rich and creamy texture when they are melted. Check the seasoning and serve.

• Serve with Nebbiolo D'Alba.

# porcini risotto

---

extra virgin olive oil for frying

400g/13oz fresh porcini, cut into 3mm/⅛in slices

600g/1¼lb risotto base (see page 94)

450ml/¾ pint vegetable stock (see page 20)

125g/4oz butter

125g/4oz freshly grated Parmesan

salt and freshly ground black pepper

---

1   Heat some olive oil in a large heavy-based frying pan and sauté the mushrooms for a few minutes. Season well.

2   Add the risotto base and the vegetable stock to the frying pan and continue to cook, stirring, for 4–5 minutes until all the liquid has been absorbed and the rice is cooked.

3   Remove the frying pan from the heat and carefully stir in the butter and Parmesan until they are melted to give a rich and creamy texture. Check the seasoning and serve.

• Serve with Nebbiolo D'Alba.

 If fresh porcini are unavailable, substitute dried porcini. You will need about one-third of the specified fresh weight and must soak the dried porcini beforehand. The water can be used in place of the same quantity of vegetable stock to cook the risotto.

# risotto with asparagus

625g/1¼lb *asparagus, trimmed, cut into stalks and tips*

*garlic oil for frying* (see page 10)

450ml/¾ pint *vegetable stock* (see page 20)

600g/1¼lb *risotto base* (see page 94)

125g/4oz *butter*

125g/4oz *freshly grated Parmesan*

*salt and freshly ground black pepper*

1  Finely chop the asparagus stalks. Heat some garlic oil in a large heavy-based frying pan and sauté the stalks for 2 minutes. Season well.

2  Add 100ml/3½fl oz of vegetable stock to the frying pan and cook for 8–10 minutes until the asparagus is soft. Allow to cool slightly, then transfer the asparagus to the bowl of a food processor fitted with the metal blade. Whiz to a fine purée.

3  Pass the asparagus through a fine sieve into a large bowl and check the seasoning.

4  Thinly slice the asparagus tips. Heat some more garlic oil in the frying pan and sauté the tips for 2 minutes. Season well.

5  Add the risotto base, the remaining vegetable stock and the asparagus purée to the frying pan and cook, stirring, for 4–5 minutes until all the liquid has been absorbed and the rice is cooked.

6  Remove the frying pan from the heat and add the butter and Parmesan, stirring well until they are completely melted and a rich and creamy texture has formed. Check the seasoning again and serve.

• *Serve with Frascati.*

# risotto primavera

275g/9oz *courgettes*

*garlic oil for frying* (see page 10)

200g/7oz *spinach, picked*

125g/4oz *broccoli, trimmed and cut into small florets*

125g/4oz *garden peas, shelled*

150g/5oz *asparagus, trimmed and thinly sliced*

125g/4oz *fava (broad) beans, shelled*

600g/1¼lb *risotto base* (see page 94)

450ml/¾ pint *vegetable stock* (see page 20)

125g/4oz *butter*

125g/4oz *freshly grated Parmesan*

*salt and freshly ground black pepper*

1  Finely chop 200g/8oz of courgettes. Heat some garlic oil in a large heavy-based frying pan and fry the courgettes, spinach and seasoning for 2 minutes until cooked. Leave to cool slightly.

2  Transfer to the bowl of a food processor fitted with the metal blade and whiz until you have a smooth purée.

3  Cut the remaining courgettes into dice of about 3mm/⅛in. Heat some more garlic oil in the frying pan and sauté the broccoli, peas, courgettes, asparagus and beans for 2 minutes until soft. Season well.

4  Add the risotto base and the vegetable stock to the frying pan and continue to cook, stirring, for 4–5 minutes until all the liquid has been absorbed and the rice is cooked.

5  Remove the frying pan from the heat and add the puréed vegetables, butter and Parmesan, stirring carefully, until the butter and Parmesan are melted and a rich and creamy texture has formed. Check the seasoning and serve.

• *Serve with Pinot Grigio.*

# risotto with seafood & saffron

100ml/3½fl oz *extra virgin olive oil*

100g/3½oz *clams, washed well*

100g/3½oz *mussels, washed well*

100g/3½oz *squid, cleaned, body sliced ino rings and tentacles halved*

8 *tiger prawns, shells on or off as preferred*

4 *langoustines, shells on or off as preferred*

2 *shallots, finely diced*

1 *bay leaf*

1 *garlic clove, crushed with salt to a purée*

pinch *saffron threads*

50ml/2fl oz *white wine*

600g/1¼lb *risotto base* (see page 94)

450ml/¾ pint *fish stock* (see page 20)

150g/5oz *butter*

*salt and freshly ground black pepper*

1 Heat the olive oil in a large, heavy-based frying pan and when hot add the clams and mussels. Cover with a lid and cook until they start to open, about 2 minutes, then add the squid, tiger prawns and langoustines and cook for a further 3 minutes.

2 Add the shallots, bay leaf, garlic and saffron threads and sauté for 3 minutes.

3 Deglaze the pan with white wine and when the liquid has reduced to almost nothing, add the the risotto base. Add the fish stock a little at a time until the liquid has been absorbed and the rice is cooked, about 5 minutes.

4 Finally, vigorously stir in the butter, season and serve.

• *Serve with Franciacorta.*

# squab & wild mushroom risotto

2 *squab, all meat removed from bones*

50g/2oz *carrots, roughly diced*

50g/2oz *leeks, outer leaves removed, thoroughly washed and roughly diced*

50g/2oz *onions, roughly diced*

50g/2oz *celery, roughly diced*

15g/½oz each *chopped thyme, oregano and marjoram*

300ml/½ pint *Barolo wine*

25ml/1fl oz *vegetable oil*

100ml/3½fl oz *tomato passata*

*salt and freshly ground black pepper*

for the risotto

200g/7oz *butter*

125g/4oz *fresh mixed wild mushrooms, such as porcini, trompettes, girolles, morelles*

600g/1¼lb *risotto base (see page 94)*

125g/4oz *freshly grated Parmesan*

for the stock

*squab bones, reserved from squab above*

50ml/2fl oz *vegetable oil*

1 bulb *garlic, cut in half*

15g/½oz *rosemary, finely chopped*

75g/3oz *carrots, roughly diced*

75g/3oz *leeks, outer leaves removed, thoroughly washed and roughly diced*

75g/3oz *celery, roughly diced*

75g/3oz *onions, roughly diced*

75ml/3fl oz *tomato passata*

1 litre/1¾ pints *water*

The squab needs to be marinated the day before, and the stock made 4 hours in advance.

1  Chop the squab meat into small pieces and marinate it with the carrots, leeks, onions, celery, herbs and wine, covered, in the refrigerator for 24 hours.

2  To make the stock, first preheat oven to 200°C (400°F), Gas Mark 5 and in a roasting tin cook the bones, uncovered, for about 40 minutes until golden brown.

3  Meanwhile, heat the vegetable oil in a large heavy-based saucepan and when hot add the garlic, rosemary, carrots, leeks, celery and onions. Sauté until all the vegetables have softened, about 10 minutes.

4  Add the passata to the saucepan and cook until the mixture has reduced by a fifth. Then add the squab bones and push them down into the liquid. Add the water and bring the stock to the boil, then simmer for 4 hours. Skim the surface of the stock occasionally to remove the excess fat.

5  Leave the stock to cool, then drain into a separate saucepan through a fine sieve.

6  Drain and set aside the wine from the marinated squab mixture.

7  To cook the squab, heat the vegetable oil in a large heavy-based frying pan. When the oil is hot add the marinated squab mixture to the pan and sauté until the meat turns golden brown, about 10 minutes.

8  Add the passata and reduce by four-fifths. Then add the reserved wine and reduce until the alcohol has burnt out, about 5 minutes.

9  Add 1 litre/1¾ pints of the stock to the frying pan and cook until the squab meat is tender, about 1 hour.

10 To make the risotto, in a large heavy-based frying pan, melt 50g/2oz butter. Add the wild mushrooms and cook until soft, about 7 minutes. Season well.

11 Stir in the prepared squab mixture and risotto base. Continue stirring, as you gradually add the remaining stock, a little at a time, until the rice is cooked and the liquid has almost disappeared, about 5 minutes.

12 Add the remaining butter and the Parmesan and stir it in to give the risotto a creamy texture. Season and serve immediately.

• *Serve with Chianti Classico.*

*Squab is a small, farmed pigeon that is bred especially for the table, giving very tender meat, but you can substitute wild pigeon if preferred.*

# polenta

200g/7oz *white polenta*

500ml/17fl oz *water*

500ml/17fl oz *milk*

1 *garlic clove, crushed with salt to a purée*

1 *bay leaf*

*salt and freshly ground black pepper*

1 Bring a large, heavy-based saucepan of salted water and milk to the boil, then reduce to a gentle simmer. Slowly pour in the polenta in a steady stream, stirring continuously.

2 Add the garlic purée and the bay leaf and leave to simmer, stirring occasionally, for about 45 minutes (the polenta becomes more dense and thicker as you stir). Season well. As the polenta has quite a neutral taste, it can take a lot of seasoning.

3 Leave the polenta to cool a little in the saucepan before serving.

• *Merlot goes well with many polenta dishes. Serve Sangiovese with the braised Umbrian lentils (right).*

 *Polenta can be served as an accompaniment to main dishes. One option is to pour the cooked polenta onto a tray while still hot, then leave it to cool and put in the refreigerator to set. Then it can be cut into squares and pan-fried for serving with meat or fish.*

# braised Umbrian lentils

200ml/7fl oz *extra virgin olive oil, plus extra for drizzling*

50g/2oz *carrots, roughly diced*

50g/2oz *leeks, outer leaves removed, thoroughly washed and roughly diced*

50g/2oz *celery, roughly diced*

50g/2oz *onions, roughly diced*

50g/2oz *garlic, crushed*

50g/2oz *pancetta*

1 *rosemary sprig*

1 *bay leaf*

1 *sage leaf*

400g/13oz *Umbrian lentils, soaked overnight*

1 litre/1¼ pints *vegetable stock* (see page 20)

25ml/1fl oz *white wine vinegar*

*salt and freshly ground black pepper*

1 Warm a large heavy-based saucepan, then add 100ml/3½fl oz olive oil. When hot, about 1 minute, add half the carrots, leeks, celery, onions, garlic, pancetta and all the herbs. Sauté, shaking the pan occasionally, for 2 minutes.

2 Stir in the lentils well. Pour in the stock and bring to the boil, then reduce to a simmer and cook until the lentils have opened, about 50 minutes. Skim away any scum that appears.

3 Meanwhile, in a frying pan, heat 100ml/3½fl oz olive oil. Add the remaining vegetables and sauté until almost soft, about 10 minutes.

4 Add the white wine vinegar and reduce until the vinegar has been absorbed by the vegetables, about 5 minutes. Add the sautéed vegetables to the lentils and season.

5 Finish off the braised lentils with a drizzle of olive oil.

# minestrone & farro soup

250ml/8fl oz *extra virgin olive oil*

1 bulb *garlic, cut in half horizontally*

125g/4oz *pancetta*

1 bunch *basil, leaves picked*

125g/4oz *onions, roughly chopped*

125g/4oz *carrots, roughly chopped*

125g/4oz *celery, roughly chopped*

200g/7oz *courgettes, roughly chopped*

200g/7oz *aubergines, roughly chopped*

200g/7oz *cavolo nero or Savoy cabbage, chopped*

10 *plum tomatoes, roughly chopped*

2 litres/3½ pints *vegetable stock* (see page 20)

1 *crusty ciabatta loaf, chopped into bite-sized pieces*

200g/7oz *freshly grated Parmesan*

200g/7oz *farro, cooked (or substitute small pasta)*

This soup should ideally be made a day in advance of serving.

1  Heat through a large heavy-based saucepan and pour in the olive oil. When hot, add the garlic, pancetta, basil, onions, carrots and celery. Sauté for 15 minutes, shaking the saucepan occasionally, then add the courgettes, aubergines and cavolo nero or Savoy cabbage. Sauté for 15 minutes, shaking the saucepan occasionally.

2  Add the tomatoes and cook for a further 15 minutes, shaking the saucepan occasionally.

3  Pour in the stock and bring to the boil, then reduce to a simmer for 30 minutes.

4  Add the ciabatta, Parmesan and farro to the soup and leave to infuse, covered, for 24 hours. Heat through before serving.

• *Serve with Merlot.*

# lentil soup

200ml/7fl oz *extra virgin olive oil,*
*plus extra for drizzling*

50g/2oz *garlic, crushed*

1 sprig each *rosemary, oregano and marjoram*

1 *bay leaf*

50g/2oz *pancetta or prosciutto hock, roughly diced*

50g/2oz *carrots, roughly diced*

50g/2oz *leeks, outer leaves removed, thoroughly washed and roughly diced*

50g/2oz *celery, roughly diced*

50g/2oz *onions, roughly diced*

75g/3oz *plum tomatoes on the vine, roughly chopped*

400g/13oz *Umbrian lentils, soaked overnight*

2 litres/3½ pints *vegetable stock* (see page 20)

*salt and freshly ground black pepper*

**for the garnish**

*freshly grated Parmesan*

1  Warm a large heavy-based saucepan and when hot add half the olive oil. Stir the garlic, herbs and pancetta or prosciutto into the oil.

2  Add the carrots, leeks, celery, onions and tomatoes and cook for 2 minutes.

3  Next, pour in the lentils and stir continuously so that they are worked into the mixture.

4  Add half the vegetable stock, bring to the boil and skim away any scum. Repeat with the remaining stock.

5  Reduce the heat to a simmer and leave the lentils to cook gently in the sauce for about 1½ hours until they are fully open.

6  Leave to cool (preferably overnight). Reheat and season. Serve in bowls with a good drizzle of oil and sprinkling of Parmesan.

• *Serve with Chianti or Montepulciano.*

# fish & seafood

crab, avocado & pepper salad

tuna carpaccio with avocado salsa

marjoram-baked halibut with braised chard

tuna with marsala, peppers & olives

salmon in pepper crust with beans & tomatoes

baked cod with broccoli & speck

monkfish with clams, girolles & leeks

pan-fried scallops with borlotti purée
    & pepper salsa

mussel & borlotti soup

roast sea bass with fennel & potatoes

roast sea bass with balsamic herb salsa

chargrilled swordfish with salmoriglio salsa

chargrilled red mullet with chard

cod wrapped in fennel & speck
    with cannellini & spinach

calamari fritti with basil mayonnaise

cod baccala with toasted focaccia

chargrilled squid & lentil salad

IF FISH ISN'T REALLY FRESH, IT ISN'T WORTH BUYING: COOK SOMETHING ELSE INSTEAD. LOOK FOR FISH WITH BRIGHT EYES, BRIGHT, DEEP PINK OR RED GILLS, AND A FIRM STIFF BODY. ABOVE ALL, A REALLY FRESH FISH SHOULDN'T SMELL FISHY. ALL YOU SHOULD SMELL IS A SUGGESTION OF THE SEA.

# fish stock
The best bones for fish stock are from flat white fish like turbot, brill and sole, not oily fish like sardines. Soak the bones in cold water first to remove excess protein and blood, which will make the stock cloudy. The recipe on page 20 is for an all-purpose fish stock which can be used in risottos, as a base for soups and sauces, or for poaching fish or ravioli of fish.

# bottarga
Traditionally bottarga is made from the salted, dried and pressed roe of grey mullet; it is also made with the roe of tuna, which is darker and drier than the superior, almost transparent amber mullet roe. For many people its intensely fishy flavour, almost like Vietnamese fish paste, is a true delicacy, but it is an aquired taste. Traditionally it is served sliced with olive oil and lemon juice on hot crusty bread, or shaved, like a white truffle, over hot pasta, with a little bit of butter.

# swordfish
Swordfish is a great favourite in the south of Italy, especially around Sicily. It is not unlike tuna, in that it is firm and meaty, but it has a more delicate flavour, and the flesh is slightly drier, which lends itself to slicing more thinly. At Daphne's it is usually served chargrilled with the traditional and intense salmoriglio salsa, made with fresh oregano, lemon juice, olive oil and lots of salt (see page 129), accompanied by a radicchio, endive and watercress salad. It is also good with fettuccine, or presented as a carpaccio, chargrilled for the briefest time, then sliced very finely onto a plate, with lemon juice, a drizzle of olive oil and a few capers.

# mussels

The best mussels are not too big, about an inch long, but meaty. Every cookery book will repeat the routine for preparing mussels, but it can't be stressed enough. You need to rinse them under cold running water and scrape away any beards — the part of the mussel which once attached it to its rock or growing post. Then rinse them at least twice more. Throw away any that are cracked or damaged, or won't close if tapped. If in any doubt, discard them anyway. Any mussels that refuse to open as they cook should also be consigned to the bin. The best mussel dishes are the simplest, such as the classic dish made with linguine. Put some olive oil in a pan, with some chopped garlic, a dash of white wine and a little saffron, bring to the boil, tip in the mussels, put a lid on tightly, and shake the pan around for a few minutes. When the mussels have opened, add some cooked linguine, shake it around again to combine the pasta with the juices and serve.

# clams (vongole)

Clams come in myriad varieties from littlenecks and cherry stones to the tender, delicately flavoured Palourdes which are the favourite at Daphne's, about three-quarters of an inch across, with a good meat to shell ratio. Like mussels, you should use only those that are tightly closed, wash them in several changes of running water, and discard any that don't open when cooked. To make a classic spaghetti vongole, heat some olive oil in a large pan, add some chopped garlic, shallots and white wine, bring to the boil, then put in the clams and cover tightly, shaking over a high heat until the shells open. Then add your cooked spaghetti or linguine, with plenty of chopped parsley, and toss well to coat the pasta with the juices.

# sea bass

Whole line-caught sea bass are huge favourites at the restaurant, expensive, but packed with flavour, with a firm, white, flaky flesh. When they are caught on lines, the fish stay more intact and are less likely to be damaged than those trawled in nets. Sea bass is at its most delicious simply barbecued or chargrilled, though one of its other charms is its diversity, so it can happily be poached, steamed or briefly pan-fried and then finished off in the oven.

# brill

Brill and turbot are very similar, both flat and white-fleshed, though turbot is larger, more knobbly in appearance and more expensive. Brill has a yielding texture and amenable flavour that readily absorbs quite dramatic flavours, so it can be paired with creamy or oil-based sauces, or vibrant salsas. It is often poached or smaller fish can be roasted on the bone. Avoid brill when it is full of roe, as there will be very little flesh for your money.

# red mullet
Another very popular fish, with its stunning pink colour, tinged with yellow, its firm, flaky texture and delicate flavour, that prefers nothing too overpowering with it. It works well with braised chard (see page 132). Red mullet is a quite small, but very bony fish, so take care when filleting it, and when serving it whole it is best to warn people to watch out for bones. Red mullet doesn't happily lend itself to poaching or steaming, and is best pan-fried, grilled or roasted in the oven. Some people consider the liver to be a delicacy and prefer it to be left in when the fish is grilled whole.

# langoustines
The best langoustines are live and twitching; frozen ones turn to cotton wool when they are thawed out. However, they can be difficult to find, because the catch is subject to the vagaries of weather, and restaurants are always clamouring for whatever is available. The simplest way to serve them is to drop them straight into a pan of boiling, salted water for 2 to 3 minutes, then peel them and eat them with nothing but a squeeze of lemon or some good mayonnaise. Or barbecue them. At Daphne's they are included in a dish of mixed seafood with spaghetti (see page 70) and occasionally chargrilled and added to risotto (see page 101).

# crab meat
Preparing whole crab demands a lot of work and patience. At Daphne's only the claws are used, from which the chunkiest and sweetest white meat is extracted. It is mixed with a little lemon or mayonnaise and served simply in salads (see page 114).

# squid
Part of the octopus and cuttlefish family, squid are known as cephalopods, the Greek for 'head on their feet', because their tentacles grow out from the head. Very large squid will usually be rubbery, however you treat them, whereas fresh baby squid are usually much more tender and are the safest bet when chargrilling or pan-frying. You can buy the squid ready-prepared (and the ink in packets) or do it yourself by putting your hand inside the body and pulling on the tentacles so that the insides come away. Next remove and discard the quill and the guts. Keep the dark ink sac if you want to use the ink to flavour a sauce or colour and flavour spaghetti or a risotto (puncture the sac to release the ink, mix it with a little water and strain before use). Wash the body, remove the fins that are attached to it, and if there is still a flimsy membrane on the outside, strip this off too. If you want to cook the tentacles along with the body, these can be cut from the head, just in front of the eyes, and the beak squeezed out and discarded. Slice the body into rings for calamari (see page 136), or cut it down the centre and open it out, then score the inside in a series of fine criss-cross cuts ready for chargrilling (see page 140).

# crab, avocado & pepper salad

300g/10oz *crabmeat, preferably white meat only*

25ml/1fl oz *lemon juice*

100ml/3½fl oz *extra virgin olive oil*

1 *red pepper, skin removed, deseeded and cut into strips*

2 *plum tomatoes, deseeded and cut into strips*

4 *basil leaves, finely shredded*

1 *avocado, peeled, halved, stone removed and cut into small dice*

50g/2oz *red onion, diced*

25ml/1fl oz *lime juice*

*salt and freshly ground black pepper*

**for the Parmesan crisps**

150g/5oz *freshly grated Parmesan*

**for the garnish**

125g/4oz *rocket*

20g/¼oz *salted capers, washed and deep-fried*

1  To make the Parmesan crisps, preheat the oven to 180°C (350°F), Gas Mark 4. Meanwhile, fill a 7cm/3in metal ring with just enough Parmesan to make a circle covering the surface of a baking tray. Make 12 circles and bake in the oven for 8 minutes. Leave to cool and transfer to a rack.

2  For the salad, pick over the crabmeat to make sure that any shell has been removed and place in a bowl. Season and add the lemon juice and half the olive oil.

3  In a separate bowl, mix the red pepper and tomatoes with the basil, seasoning and a quarter of the remaining oil.

4  In another bowl, mix the avocado with the red onion, lime juice and seasoning.

5  To serve, place a Parmesan crisp in the centre of each plate, then top with the avocado mixture. Add another crisp and top with the crab mixture. Finally, add another crisp and top with the tomato/pepper mixture.

6  In a bowl, toss the rocket in the remaining olive oil and use it to garnish each plate. Scatter capers around the rocket and serve.

• *Serve with Verdicchio Classico.*

# tuna carpaccio with avocado salsa

*250g/8oz fresh tuna loin, skin removed, cleaned*

*sea salt and freshly ground black pepper*

*for the salsa*

*2 avocados, halved, stone removed, peeled and diced*

*juice of 2 limes*

*25ml/1fl oz extra virgin olive oil, plus extra for garnish*

*1 red chilli, deseeded and finely chopped*

*20g/¼oz coriander, finely chopped*

*salt and freshly ground black pepper*

*for the garnish*

*2 limes, cut in half*

For this dish, the tuna loin needs to be prepared at least 24 hours in advance of the main recipe.

1  On a work surface, roll the tuna in black pepper. Heat a large heavy-based dry frying pan and sear the tuna quickly on both sides, about 2 minutes.

2  Remove the tuna from the frying pan and roll it up tightly in plastic wrap. Leave to cool, then refrigerate for at least 24 hours.

3  To make the salsa, place the avocados in a large bowl. Add the lime juice, olive oil, chilli and coriander. Mix all the ingredients together and season to taste.

4  To serve, remove tuna from refrigerator and slice very thinly with a very sharp knife. The slices should be almost transparent. Arrange overlapping slices on each plate to form a large circle. Spoon the salsa into the centre, place half a lime on top, season with sea salt and drizzle a little olive oil over the top.

• *Serve with Chardonnay.*

# marjoram-baked halibut with braised chard

50ml/2fl oz *extra virgin olive oil*

125g/4oz *cipolline (baby onions), finely sliced*

20g/¾oz *marjoram, freshly picked (if possible) and finely chopped*

20g/¾oz *oregano, freshly picked (if possible) and finely chopped*

juice of 1 *lemon*

4 x 200g/7oz *halibut fillets*

50ml/2fl oz *garlic oil* (see page 10)

400g/13oz *Swiss red chard, roughly chopped*

*salt and freshly ground black pepper*

1 *lemon, cut into wedges*

1 Preheat oven to 190°C (375°F), Gas Mark 5. Heat half the olive oil in a large heavy-based frying pan. Add the cipolline and cook until they are transparent and without colour.

2 In a shallow bowl, mix the herbs, the remaining olive oil and the lemon juice (reserve a little to squeeze over the salad) together.

3 Coat the top of the halibut with the herb mixture and bake in the oven for 6–7 minutes until just firm but very moist.

4 Meanwhile, in a large heavy-based frying pan heat the garlic oil, add the cooked cipolline and the Swiss chard. Toss together and season. Add a squeeze of lemon juice.

5 Divide the chard among the plates, place a baked halibut fillet on top and finish with a wedge of lemon.

• *Serve with Meursault or other dry French white.*

# tuna with marsala, peppers & olives

100ml/3½fl oz *extra virgin olive oil,*

*plus extra for drizzling*

1 *garlic clove, crushed with salt to a purée*

1 *rosemary sprig, leaves picked and finely chopped*

2 *red onions, finely sliced*

4 x 200g/7oz *tuna steaks*

2 *red peppers, skins removed, deseeded and*

*thinly sliced*

2 *yellow peppers, skins removed, deseeded and*

*thinly sliced*

60g/2½oz *black olives, pitted*

100ml/3½fl oz *Marsala*

200ml/7fl oz *tomato sauce* (see page 25)

16 *basil leaves, freshly picked (if possible) and*

*torn in half*

*salt and freshly ground black pepper*

**for the garnish**

1 *rosemary sprig, leaves picked*

1 Preheat oven to 180°C (350°F), Gas Mark 4. Gently heat a little of the olive oil in a large heavy-based frying pan. Add the garlic purée, rosemary and red onions and sauté, shaking the pan occasionally, until they are soft but without colour, about 8 minutes.

2 Season the tuna steaks. Warm a little olive oil in a large deep casserole until smoking, about 5 minutes. Add the tuna steaks and cook for about 3 minutes until golden brown, then turn them over. Place the peppers, sautéed red onions and black olives around the outside of the steaks and bake in the oven for 3 minutes.

3 Remove the fish from the casserole and place in the centre of a deep serving plate. Keep warm.

4 Deglaze the casserole with Marsala and when the alcohol has burnt out, about 4 minutes, add the tomato sauce and torn basil. Cook for a further minute and check the seasoning.

5 Pour the sauce over the top of the fish and finish with a drizzle of olive oil. Garnish with the rosemary leaves and serve immediately.

• *Serve with Chardonnay.*

 *To peel peppers, place them whole under a preheated grill until they blacken, turning occasionally, about 10–12 minutes. Remove from the grill and cover with a damp cloth or wrap in plastic until the peppers cool. The skin can then be pulled or peeled off. Alternatively, preheat the oven to 180°C (350°F), Gas Mark 4 and place the peppers on a baking sheet. Drizzle with oil and bake until brown, about 15 minutes, then peel the skin in the same way.*

# salmon in pepper crust with beans & tomatoes

50ml/2fl oz *extra virgin olive oil*

1 *onion, finely diced*

50ml/2fl oz *white wine vinegar*

4 x 200g/7oz *salmon fillets, skinned and pinboned (your fishmonger can do this for you)*

15g/½oz *butter*

50ml/2fl oz *anchovy oil (see page 13)*

80g/3¼oz *cherry tomatoes, cut in half*

200g/7oz *French beans, split in half lengthways and blanched in boiling salted water for 4 minutes*

*salt and freshly ground black pepper*

**for the pepper crust**

125g/4oz *fresh breadcrumbs*

1 *red pepper, skin removed and deseeded*

½ *egg white*

1 Preheat oven to 180°C (350°F), Gas Mark 4. Meanwhile, in a large heavy-based frying pan heat half the olive oil. Add the onions and sauté until soft, about 8 minutes, shaking the pan occasionally. Deglaze with white wine vinegar, remove onions and reserve.

2 To make the pepper crust, put the breadcrumbs and red pepper in the bowl of a food processor fitted with the metal blade. Whiz until the breadcrumbs become fine and take on a reddish tinge. Add the egg white and whiz for 5 seconds more. Transfer to a large shallow bowl.

3 Season the salmon fillets and then dip them in the breadcrumb mixture.

4 Heat a large heavy-based baking dish and in it melt a knob of butter with the remaining olive oil. Place the salmon fillets in the dish, presentation side down, and bake, uncovered, in the oven for 4 minutes and then turn over. Continue baking for a further 3 minutes until the fillets are pink.

5 Meanwhile, in the heavy-based pan used previously, gently heat the anchovy oil. Add the cherry tomatoes and sauté until soft, about 3 minutes, shaking the saucepan occasionally.

6 Add the prepared onions and French beans and cook together until hot, about 3 minutes. Season well.

7 To serve, put some of the bean/tomato mixture in the centre of each plate and place a salmon fillet on top.

• *Serve with Pouilly Fuissé.*

# baked cod with broccoli & speck

150g/5oz *purple sprouting broccoli*
*(if unavailable, use ordinary broccoli)*

50ml/2fl oz *extra virgin olive oil,*
*plus extra for drizzling*

4 x 200g/7oz *cod fillets, pinboned and with the*
*skin still on (your fishmonger can do this for you)*

300ml/½ *pint veal stock* (see page 21)

50ml/2fl oz *garlic oil* (see page 10)

50g/2oz *speck (use pancetta, if unavailable)*

40g/1½oz *baby onions, sautéed until softened in*
*extra virgin olive oil*

60g/2¼oz *fava (broad) beans, shelled*

40g/1½oz *garden peas, shelled*

*juice of 1 lemon*

*salt and freshly ground black pepper*

1  Preheat oven to 190°C (375°F), Gas Mark 5. Trim the broccoli, cut the heads into small florets and finely slice the stems. Blanch in boiling salted water until al dente, about 3 minutes. Set aside.

2  Heat a large heavy-based casserole and add 50ml/2fl oz of olive oil. When smoking, about 1 minute, place the cod in the casserole, skin side down. Season well and bake in the oven uncovered for 4 minutes until slightly firm.

3  While the cod is baking, in a large heavy-based saucepan heat the veal stock through and reduce by three-quarters. Keep warm.

4  In a large heavy-based frying pan, heat the garlic oil and add the speck or pancetta and then the broccoli and the baby onions. Sauté for 2 minutes, shaking the pan occasionally.

5  Add the fava beans and peas to the frying pan and check the seasoning. Keep warm.

6  Turn the cod fillets over and bake for a further 2 minutes. Remove from the oven and squeeze the lemon juice over the fish.

7  To serve, put some broccoli in the centre of each plate and place the cod on top, skin side up. Drizzle veal stock around the outside of the plates and finally drizzle extra virgin olive oil over the veal stock.

• *Serve with Chablis.*

# monkfish with clams, girolles & leeks

4 x 200g/7oz *monkfish, cleaned of sinew and blood,*
*skinned and descaled (your fishmonger can do this)*

*plain flour for coating*

*extra virgin olive oil for frying*

1 *carrot, roughly chopped*

50g/2oz *onions, roughly chopped*

50g/2oz *celery, roughly chopped*

1 *garlic clove, crushed*

8 *sage leaves*

24 *clams, washed well*

200ml/7fl oz *white wine*

*salt and freshly ground black pepper*

**for the girolle & leek mixture**

250ml/8fl oz *monkfish stock (follow recipe for fish*
*stock on page 20, using monkfish bones, trimmings)*

300g/10oz *butter*

*juice of 1 lemon*

200g/7oz *baby leeks, outer leaves removed, trimmed,*
*washed, then blanched in just enough water to cover*
*them for 1 minute*

200g/7oz *girolles, cleaned, stem scraped and sautéed in*
*a knob of butter until soft*

2 *tomatoes, peeled, deseeded and cut into fine dice*

20g/¼oz *flat-leaf parsley, finely shredded*

1 Preheat oven to 190°C (375°F), Gas Mark 5. Season the monkfish well, coat them in flour and shake off the excess.

2 Warm a large ovenproof frying pan and add enough oil to cover the base. When smoking, seal the monkfish fillets on both sides.

3 Use a fish slice to transfer the monkfish to a plate. Add the carrot, onions, celery, garlic and sage leaves to the frying pan. Place the monkfish on top and bake in the oven for 6–7 minutes until just firm but still very moist. Remove pan from the oven and leave to stand for 2 minutes. Keep fish warm and discard the vegetables.

4 Meanwhile, heat a large heavy-based saucepan until hot, then add the clams, cover with a lid and cook for 1 minute.

5 Add the wine and reduce. When the alcohol has burnt out, the clams should be open. Remove from the pan (discarding any clams that are closed) and transfer to a plate. Keep warm.

6 Add half the monkfish stock to the saucepan and reduce until the stock begins to caramelise (this will produce a nuttier taste). Then add the remaining fish stock and reduce by half.

7 Whisk in the butter, reserving a knob for later, and add the lemon juice.

8 Add the blanched leeks, sautéed girolles, tomatoes and parsley and bring the mixture to almost boiling point. Check the seasoning and consistency (it should be quite thin) and stir in a knob of butter.

9 To serve, place some clams in the centre of each plate with some of the girolle and leek mixture. Arrange the monkfish on top and finish with the remaining girolles and leeks.

• *Serve with Pinot Grigio.*

# pan-fried scallops with borlotti purée & pepper salsa

*extra virgin olive oil for frying*

*12 scallops, use the meat only (the roe can also be included, if liked)*

*1 lemon, cut in half*

*salt and freshly ground black pepper*

**for the borlotti purée**

*100ml/3½fl oz extra virgin olive oil*

*150g/5oz mirepoix (1 leek, outer leaves removed and washed, 1 carrot, 1 celery stick and 1 onion, roughly chopped)*

*1 bay leaf*

*4 garlic cloves, crushed with salt to a purée*

*400g/13oz borlotti beans, soaked overnight*

*1 litre/1¼ pints vegetable stock (see page 20)*

*red pepper trimmings from the salsa (see below)*

**for the pepper salsa**

*4 plum tomatoes, skinned, deseeded and quartered*

*100ml/3½fl oz extra virgin olive oil*

*½ chilli, deseeded and finely chopped*

*1 garlic clove, crushed with salt to a purée*

*100ml/3½fl oz red wine vinegar*

*½ red onion, finely diced*

*1 red pepper, skinned, deseeded and finely diced*

*1 yellow pepper, skinned, deseeded and finely diced*

*50g/2oz capers, rinsed well under cold water*

*10 basil leaves, torn*

*50g/2oz flat-leaf parsley, finely shredded*

**for the leek garnish**

*extra virgin olive oil for deep-frying*

*1 leek, outer leaves removed, thoroughly washed and cut into julienne strips of about 7cm/3in*

1  To make the borlotti purée, heat the olive oil in a large heavy-based frying pan. Add the mirepoix, bay leaf and garlic purée. Sauté for 2 minutes, shaking the pan occasionally.

2  Add the borlotti beans and stir in well. Then add the stock and bring to the boil, stirring.

3  Add the red pepper trimmings to the mixture. Reduce to a simmer and when all the ingredients are fully cooked and the liquid has been absorbed, about 1 hour, place the mixture in the bowl of a blender or food processor fitted with the metal blade and whiz until a purée is formed, about 2–3 minutes.

4  While the beans are cooking, begin the pepper salsa. Lay the tomatoes on a baking sheet, then season well and leave to infuse for an hour.

5  When the tomatoes are ready, heat the olive oil in a large heavy-based frying pan. When hot, about 2 minutes, add the chilli, garlic and onion. Soften, stirring occasionally, about 7–8 minutes. Add the red wine vinegar and reduce until it has been absorbed, about 5 minutes.

6  Add the mixed peppers to the saucepan and cook, stirring occasionally, for 5 minutes.

7  Pour the infused tomatoes over the top and mix together. Add the capers, basil and parsley, then check the seasoning.

8  For the garnish, warm enough olive oil to deep-fry the leeks in a small heavy-based saucepan. Fry the leeks, shaking the saucepan occasionally, until they are crispy but still green, about 3 minutes. Drain on kitchen paper. (The same can be done with strips of aubergine skin if desired.)

9  To serve, warm a large heavy-based frying pan and add enough olive oil to cover the base. Season the scallops and pan-fry them for 45 seconds on each side.

10  Place some salsa in the middle of each plate and make a well in the centre to hold a portion of purée. Add a squeeze of lemon juice to the scallops and sit them on top. Garnish the scallops with a cluster of deep-fried leeks.

• *Serve with Chardonnay or Sauvignon Blanc.*

# mussel & borlotti soup

200ml/7fl oz *extra virgin olive oil*

400g/13oz *mussels, beards removed and washed well*

1 *chilli, deseeded and finely chopped*

1 *garlic clove, crushed*

1 *rosemary sprig, leaves picked and finely chopped*

125g/4oz *celery, cut into chunks (leaves reserved)*

125g/4oz *leeks, outer leaves removed, thoroughly washed and cut into chunks*

125g/4oz *carrots, cut into chunks*

125g/4oz *onions, cut into chunks*

200ml/7fl oz *tomato passata*

1 litre/1¾ *pints fish stock* (see page 20)

500g/1lb *borlotti beans, soaked overnight and boiled in vegetable stock or water for 1 hour, then drained*

*handful celery leaves, finely shredded (reserved from celery above)*

*salt and freshly ground black pepper*

1 Warm a large heavy-based saucepan and when hot add the olive oil and warm through, about 2 minutes. Add the mussels and cover with a lid. Cook until the mussels open, about 5 minutes, shaking the saucepan occasionally.

2 Remove the mussels from the saucepan with a slotted spoon, discarding any that have not opened, and transfer to a large bowl. Cover tightly with plastic wrap and set aside.

3 Add the chilli, garlic, rosemary, celery, leeks, carrots and onions to the saucepan and cook until soft, about 10 minutes, shaking the saucepan occasionally.

4 Next, stir in the passata and reduce the mixture by half. Add the fish stock and slowly bring to the boil, stirring.

5 Place one-third of the cooked beans in the bowl of a food processor fitted with the metal blade. Whiz to form a fine purée, about 3 minutes.

6 Add the purée and the rest of the whole cooked beans to the soup and leave to simmer for 30 minutes, stirring occasionally.

7 Add the mussels to the soup (in or out of their shells, as desired) and cook for 5 minutes.

8 Season, then garnish with celery leaves and serve in deep bowls.

• *Serve with Chablis.*

# roast sea bass with fennel & potatoes

100ml/3½fl oz *clarified butter* (see method)

4 x 500g/1lb *sea bass, descaled, gutted and fins removed (your fishmonger can do this for you)*

1 *garlic clove*

100ml/3½fl oz *extra virgin olive oil, plus extra for drizzling*

200g/7oz *new potatoes, peeled and cut in half lengthwise*

1 *onion, thinly sliced*

4 heads of *fennel, cut into wedges*

20g/¾oz *flat-leaf parsley, fnely shredded*

*salt and freshly ground black pepper*

1  Preheat oven to 190°C (375°F), Gas Mark 5. Meanwhile, clarify the butter by heating it gently until melted, then remove from heat and allow to cool. Ladle out the impurities, leaving the clear butter behind, and reserve.

2  Season the sea bass, inside and out, and place it on a baking tray with the garlic clove. Drizzle with olive oil and wrap in foil.

3  Bake the fish in the oven for 12 minutes. Remove tray from oven. Remove garlic clove and press to remove puréed flesh and reserve. Leave fish to rest for 5 minutes, then remove skin and, if desired, bones. Keep the fish warm. Reduce oven temperature to 180°C (350°F), Gas Mark 4.

4  In a large heavy-based frying pan, heat the olive oil and clarified butter together. Add the new potatoes and garlic purée and sauté for about 8 minutes until coloured.

5  Add the onion slices and continue to sauté until soft, then add the fennel and sauté until soft, about 9–10 minutes.

6  Season the vegetables well and bake on a tray in the oven for 20 minutes until cooked.

7  To serve, toss the parsley through the vegetables. Place a portion of sea bass on each plate, accompanied by the vegetable mixture. Drizzle any excess liquid from the cooked vegetables over the sea bass.

• *Serve with Chardonnay or Sauvignon Blanc.*

# roast sea bass with balsamic herb salsa

475g/15oz *sea bass, scaled and gutted*
*(your fishmonger can do this for you)*
*extra virgin olive oil for brushing*
*salt and freshly ground black pepper*

*for the salsa*

juice of 1 *lemon*

100ml/3½fl oz *8-year-old balsamic vinegar*

100ml/3½fl oz *vegetable stock (see page 20)*

300ml/½ pint *extra virgin olive oil*

1 handful *chives, cut into 2½cm/1in lengths*

1 handful *rosemary, chopped*

The salsa for this recipe needs to be made 24 hours in advance of preparing the main dish.

1  To make the salsa, whisk all the liquid ingredients together in a large bowl. Season to taste. Add the herbs and leave to infuse, covered, overnight in the refrigerator.

2  Preheat oven to 190°C (375°F), Gas Mark 5. Season the fish, inside and out, with salt and pepper. Place it on an oiled baking sheet and brush with olive oil. Roast the fish, uncovered, for about 15 minutes, until cooked through (it should flake easily).

3  With a knife, gently scrape the skin away from the fish. Transfer the fish to a serving plate. Whisk up the salsa (leaving the herbs in it) and pour a generous ladleful over the fish.

• *Serve with a Sardinian white like Le Arenarie.*

# chargrilled swordfish with salmoriglio salsa

400g/13oz *swordfish loin, skinned and cleaned of any blood, then thinly sliced (your fishmonger can do this for you)*
*extra virgin olive oil for brushing*
*salt and freshly ground black pepper*

*for the salsa*

1 tsp *finely chopped fresh oregano leaves*

100ml/3½fl oz *extra virgin olive oil*

juice of 1 *lemon*

10 *mint leaves, finely chopped*

*for the salad*

125g/4oz *rocket, finely shredded*

125g/4oz *radicchio, finely shredded*

juice of 1 *lemon*

100ml/3½fl oz *extra virgin olive oil*

1  To make the salsa, mix all the ingredients together in a large bowl and season. Set aside.

2  For the salad, toss all the ingredients together in a large bowl. Season to taste and set aside.

3  Season the swordfish and brush with olive oil. Chargrill, or grill, on both sides until cooked, about 4 minutes.

4  To serve, place a little salad in the centre of each plate and top with a portion of the swordfish loin. Place some salsa around the outside of the plate and brush the swordfish with a little olive oil.

• *Serve with Orvieto Classico.*

CHARGRILLED
SWORDFISH WITH
SALMORIGLIO SALSA

# chargrilled red mullet with chard

50ml/2fl oz *extra virgin olive oil, plus extra for drizzling*

125g/4oz *onions, finely diced*

2 tsps *white wine vinegar*

4 x 250g/8oz *fillets of red mullet, descaled and pinboned (your fishmonger can do this for you)*

*plain flour for coating*

50ml/2fl oz *anchovy oil* (see page 13)

50ml/2fl oz *garlic oil* (see page 10)

400g/13oz *Swiss chard, roughly chopped*

juice of 1 *lemon*

*salt and freshly ground black pepper*

 *When chargrilling or grilling fish, always make sure you get the grill very, very hot in advance, or the skin of the fish will stick to it and spoil the dish.*

1 Warm a large heavy-based frying pan and add the olive oil. When hot add the onions and cook until soft and without colour.

2 Pour in the white wine vinegar and reduce until the liquid has evaporated, about 3 minutes. Set aside and leave to cool.

3 Season the red mullet and lightly coat with flour, shaking off any excess.

4 Pour the anchovy oil into a shallow bowl. Dip the red mullet into the oil to coat the fillets all over, then chargrill, or grill, for 3 minutes on both sides.

5 Meanwhile, in a large heavy-based frying pan, heat the garlic oil and add the chard. Fry quickly, tossing the pan occasionally, until the chard starts to go limp. Add the onions, then check the taste and season as necessary.

6 Once the mullet is grilled, give it a squeeze of lemon juice.

7 To serve, put some chard in the centre of each plate. Place a fillet of mullet on top and finish off with a drizzle of olive oil.

• *Serve with Australian Chardonnay.*

# cod wrapped in fennel & speck with cannellini & spinach

200g/7oz *speck (or pancetta or prosciutto), very thinly sliced into long strips*

200g/7oz *baby fennel, blanched in boiling water for 4 minutes, then plunged into cold water*

4 x 250g/8oz *cod fillets, skinned, descaled and pinboned (your fishmonger can do this for you)*

*salt and freshly ground black pepper*

*extra virgin olive oil for baking*

**for the cannellini bean mixture**

50ml/2fl oz *garlic oil (see page 10)*

80g/3¼oz *plum tomatoes, skinned, deseeded and finely diced*

80g/3¼oz *baby spinach*

80g/3¼oz *cannellini beans, cooked (see page 92)*

**for the red wine garnish**

15g/½oz *butter*

50g/2oz *shallots, finely diced*

1 *garlic clove, crushed*

15g/½oz *rosemary, leaves picked*

400ml/14fl oz *red wine*

1  Preheat oven to 190°C (375°F), Gas Mark 5. Meanwhile, top and tail each fennel. Separate stalks from bulbs and cut bulbs in half lengthwise and stalks in half widthwise. On a work surface lay out 4 portions of speck wide enough to cover each cod fillet and about 3 times as long. (If necessary overlap a few pieces of speck to achieve the required width.) Place a quarter of the fennel segments widthwise across each portion of speck about a third of the way up. Lay a fillet of cod on top of the fennel, skin side down, season with black pepper and roll the speck around to make a parcel.

2  Warm a large casserole with enough olive oil to cover the base. Add the cod parcels and bake in the oven for 6–8 minutes, turning the cod halfway through.

3  Meanwhile, to make the cannellini bean mixture, heat a large heavy-based frying pan and add the garlic oil. When hot, add the tomatoes and season. Sauté for 3 minutes, shaking the pan occasionally, until soft.

4  Add the baby spinach and allow to wilt, shaking the pan occasionally. Then add the cannellini beans and mix together well. Check the seasoning. Keep warm.

5  Warm another large frying pan for the red wine garnish and add a knob of butter. When the butter has melted, add the shallots, garlic and rosemary. Sauté until soft, about 6 minutes.

6  Add the red wine and reduce by four-fifths, then pass the mixture through a fine sieve into a large bowl.

7  To serve, put some cannellini mixture in the centre of each plate and place a cod parcel on top. Drizzle a thin ribbon of the red wine mixture around the outside of each plate.

• *Serve with Sauvignon Blanc.*

# calamari fritti with basil mayonnaise

100ml/3½fl oz *milk*

400g/13oz *calamari rings (squid should be washed,*
*skin and tentacles removed and body cut into rings)*

*seasoned flour for coating*

*vegetable oil for deep-frying*

1 *lemon, cut into quarters*

*basil mayonnaise* (see page 25)

1 Pour the milk into a shallow dish and then dip the calamari into it. Coat with seasoned flour and deep-fry in oil at 180°C (350°F) until golden brown, about 2–3 minutes. Drain on kitchen paper.

2 Place a portion of calamari and a lemon wedge on each plate. Serve with basil mayonnaise.

• *Serve with French Chardonnay.*

 *Whether you choose to use a large squid or a small one for this recipe is down to personal taste. The smaller variety tends to give tender calamari.*

# cod baccala with toasted focaccia

500g/1lb *cod fillets, skinned, descaled and pinboned*
*(your fishmonger can do this for you)*

1 *rosemary sprig, chopped*

1 *thyme sprig, chopped*

1 *juniper berry, crushed*

600ml/1 pint *milk*

1 *garlic clove*

400g/13oz *potatoes, peeled and cut into even pieces*

½ bunch *flat-leaf parsley, finely chopped*

200ml/7fl oz *extra virgin olive oil*

*toasted focaccia, to serve*

*salt and freshly ground black pepper*

You will need to prepare the cod for this recipe 1 day in advance of cooking.

1  Reserve 50g/2oz cod fillet and lay the remaining fish on a baking sheet. In a small bowl, mix together a pinch of sea salt with the rosemary, thyme and juniper berry. Scatter this over the top of the fish. Cover in plastic wrap and leave to infuse for 24 hours in the refrigerator.

2  Scrape the sea salt mixture away from the cod and gently rinse it under cold water for 1 minute to remove any remaining salt.

3  Place the cod in a shallow baking pan with the milk and add the garlic. Bring the milk to the boil and then remove the pan from the heat. Set aside to cool.

4  When the milk has cooled, drain it into a saucepan. Add the potatoes to the saucepan and cook them in the milk. (When cooked, the potatoes will be soft and the milk will have reduced away.)

5  While the potatoes are hot, use a fork or potato masher to mash them in the saucepan together with the cooked cod fillet and parsley.

6  Return the saucepan to a gentle heat, stirring continuously. Mix in the olive oil. Add as little or as much olive oil as you like, depending on the consistency you prefer. Then check the seasoning. The mash will now be pale green.

7  Immediately add the reserved raw cod fillet and stir it in to the green cod mash. (The raw fish will cook in the hot mash.) Season with black pepper only.

8  Serve immediately with toasted focaccia.

• *Serve with wood-aged Soave Classico.*

# chargrilled squid & lentil salad

400g/13oz *squid, ink sacs removed, cleaned, sliced lengthways to open into 1 large piece of squid, scored in a criss-cross pattern (your fishmonger can do this)*

200g/7oz *lentils, soaked overnight*

150ml/¼ pint *extra virgin olive oil*

1 *garlic clove*

50g/2oz *pancetta, thinly sliced*

1 litre/1¼ pints *vegetable stock (see page 20)*

1 *bouquet garni*

1 *red onion, very finely diced*

1 bunch *flat-leaf parsley, finely shredded*

25ml/1fl oz *red wine vinegar*

125g/4oz *rocket, freshly picked (if possible)*

4 *plum tomatoes, deseeded and diced*

juice of 2 *lemons*

*salt and freshly ground black pepper*

**for the marinade**

1 *garlic clove, crushed*

1 *chilli, deseeded and diced*

50ml/2fl oz *extra virgin olive oil*

You will need to soak the lentils for 24 hours, and marinate the squid for 2 hours, in advance of preparing the main recipe.

1  To marinate the squid, place it in a dish with 1 garlic clove, the chilli and the olive oil. Leave, covered, in the refrigerator.

2  To prepare the salad, drain the lentils and wash them thoroughly. Heat 50ml/2fl oz olive oil in a large heavy-based frying pan. Add the garlic, pancetta and then the lentils. Sauté for 5 minutes, stirring the contents of the frying pan continuously.

3  Add the vegetable stock and bouquet garni to the pan and simmer until the lentils are soft, about 45 minutes. Drain away excess liquid.

4  When the lentils are drained, transfer to a large bowl and mix in the red onion and half the parsley. Finish off by stirring in the red wine vinegar and 50ml/2fl oz extra virgin olive oil and season well.

5  To serve, toss the rocket in the remaining extra virgin olive oil, season, and arrange around the edge of each plate. Place the lentils in the middle of the leaves.

6  Place some tomato on top of the rocket to garnish the salad.

7  Chargrill, or grill, the squid until cooked, about 1 minute each side. Cut the squid into thin strips and place in a bowl. Add seasoning, lemon juice and the remaining parsley; mix together.

8  Serve the squid on top of the lentils.

• *Serve with Franciacorta Bianco.*

# poultry, meat & game

coppa with baby artichoke shavings,
   olives & lemon

beef carpaccio with truffle cheese

rump of lamb with artichoke mash
   & tomato & olive compote

liver Veneziana

pan-fried foie gras with artichoke röstis,
   cipolline & balsamic dressing

roast guinea fowl with Vin Santo & grapes

braised lamb shank with fava bean mash

chargrilled chicken with porcini

herb-crusted rack of lamb with courgettes,
   fava beans, pancetta & mint

beef tagliata with tomato, aubergine
   & basil compote

costaletta Milanese

seared foie gras with endive, pear & Vin Santo

 SALUMI, PARTICULARLY PANCETTA AND PROSCIUTTO, ARE FUNDAMENTAL ELEMENTS OF THE DAPHNE'S KITCHEN. FRESH MEAT AND GAME ARE TREATED IN THE SAME WAY AS FISH: THE CONCENTRATION IS ON QUALITY INGREDIENTS, WHICH ARE PREPARED AND SERVED VERY SIMPLY.

# pork fat
Though the lightness of cooking with olive oil is much more in tune with the Daphne's style, there are a few dishes, such as liver Veneziana (see page 155), that gain a huge depth of flavour from being cooked in the traditional way with pork fat which has been cubed and rendered down in a little water for a few hours with some herbs. Trimmings of prosciutto can be used in the same way. If you were feeling indulgent you could also use pork fat to sauté the vegetables and pancetta at the start of the braised lentil dish on page 104.

# coppa
Coppa is boned neck and shoulder of pork which has been cured in salt, pepper and nutmeg, wrapped in a cloth soaked in white wine and aged for several months. It is a well-marbled meat that looks quite fatty, but the flavour — similar to that of prosciutto — is fabulous. In Italy, pigs tend to be farmed primarily for cured meats like this, rather than for fresh meat, and it shows in the quality of the resulting product. Coppa is delicious served very simply with olive oil, lemon and black pepper and some shaved baby artichoke hearts (see page 148).

# pancetta
This is cured streaky belly bacon and can be used in any recipe that calls for bacon, provided you like the richer, slightly smokier flavour it imparts. It is one of the most versatile of Italian salumi; it can be thinly sliced and baked until crispy, sautéed with vegetables for making soups or casseroles, or used to wrap scallops before grilling.

**speck** More rustic than pancetta, speck is the cured pork produced in the mountain villages in the north-east of Italy, particularly in the region of Trentino-Alto Adige, where the close proximity of Austria exerts its influence on the local cuisine. The hind legs of the pig are cured in salt, pepper, juniper and bay, then smoked over oak and juniper berries. The result is an intense, smoky flavour that can be delicious when sliced and eaten with home-baked bread, but may be overpowering when added to some dishes, so use it sparingly.

**prosciutto** The best examples of this famous cured ham are prosciutto di Parma and prosciutto di San Daniele, which is produced in the Alps near the Austrian border. Both of these lean, sweet hams are salted and air-dried for about a year to mature. Prosciutto of this quality is best served very simply, and sliced as thinly as possible. Thick-cut prosciutto loses a great deal of charm. A quite rare and prized delicacy, rump of prosciutto, known as culatello, is produced in the Bassa Parmense, north of Parma, where it is marinated and aged in very limited quantities to produce ham with a very refined, intensely sweet flavour.

**veal** Italians have always loved veal, and its clean, simple flavour shouldn't be masked with rich or over-complicated ones. It lends itself best to classical treatment, such as being batted out flat and coated in egg and breadcrumbs for costaletta Milanese (see page 167), which is served the traditional way with spaghetti, tomato and basil. (For this dish, make up a cherry tomato sauce [see box, page 25] throw in a large handful of torn basil leaves and mix through cooked spaghetti.) Veal is also good chargrilled with fresh porcini and served with artichokes, lemon and olive oil.

**lamb** Only the best end or rump of lamb is used at Daphne's, and it is always served pink. It is important not to trim the fat before cooking, as this will baste the meat and keep it tender and juicy. Always rest lamb before serving, so that the juices can run through it and tenderise the meat.

# rabbit
Rabbit is one of the favourite game meats of Tuscany, where it is frequently stewed, perhaps with olives and tomatoes, and served as it is or shredded with pappardelle (see page 67). It has a mild, delicate taste very similar to chicken — though wild rabbit has a deeper flavour — and can be treated in much the same way.

# guinea fowl
If you are looking for a bird with a little more depth and character than chicken, substitute guinea fowl, which has a little more gaminess about it, while retaining a certain finesse. It is delicious roasted with grapes and Vin Santo, a sherry-like wine whose flavour is derived from grapes hung to dry in lofts before fermentation (see page 159).

# duck
The type of duck you need to buy will vary according to what you want to do with it. For confit, for example, you need a big fat duck leg, substantial enough to stay moist, with thick and heavy breasts. A Gressingham duck has less fat on the breast and is best for roasting, in risotto, or simply pan-fried, sliced, and served well seasoned with lemon and olive oil.

# suckling pig
This is a big Italian favourite for festivals and holidays, when the cavity of the piglet, usually about two months old and weighing about 15kg, will often be stuffed with onions and herbs, and the pig spit-roasted over several hours. At Daphne's it is something that is done on special occasions. Spit-roasted suckling pig is extremely succulent and juicy, with a lovely caramelised crackling, encasing meat so tender and melting it could almost be eaten with a spoon.

# coppa with baby artichoke shavings, olives & lemon

150g/5oz *baby artichokes*

juice of 1 *lemon*

40ml/1⅓fl oz *extra virgin olive oil*

20g/¾oz *parsley, finely chopped*

1 *red chilli, deseeded and finely chopped*

1 *lemon*

250g/8oz *coppa*

80g/3¼oz *black olives, pitted*

handful *celery leaves*

*salt and freshly ground black pepper*

 *The sharpness of the black olives is an ideal counterpoint to the artichokes. For the best flavour, buy olives with the stones in and pit them yourself.*

The artichokes used in this recipe should ideally be prepared the day before.

1 Remove the outer leaves and stems from the baby artichokes. Cut them in half lengthwise and discard the chokes from the middle. Slice the artichokes very thinly to resemble shavings.

2 In a large bowl, mix the artichoke shavings with the lemon juice, extra virgin olive oil, parsley and chilli. Season well and leave to marinate, covered, in the refrigerator for a few hours, or preferably overnight.

3 To serve, cut the whole lemon into 4 wedges. Thinly slice the coppa and arrange it so that it covers each plate. Scatter the marinated artichokes, black olives and celery leaves on top. Finally, garnish by placing a lemon wedge on top of each salad.

• *Serve with Chardonnay.*

# beef carpaccio with truffle cheese

150g/5oz *rocket*

50ml/2fl oz *lemon & olive oil dressing* (see page 24)

125g/4oz *truffle cheese*

200g/7oz *trimmed beef fillet, sliced paper-thin*

*salt and freshly ground black pepper*

*for the garnish*

*truffle oil for drizzling*

1  In a large bowl, coat the rocket with the lemon & olive oil dressing.

2  Season the beef slices and arrange a layer of them on each plate. Place a mound of rocket in the middle and shave a few slices of truffle cheese over the top.

3  To serve, drizzle over a little truffle oil and finish with a twist of black pepper.

• *Serve with Rubesco.*

*Truffle cheese is a seasonal speciality of Alba, where grated white truffles are incorporated into a semi-hard cheese. If unavailable, substitute Parmesan.*

# rump of lamb with artichoke mash & tomato & olive compote

4 x 250g/8oz *rumps of lamb*

25ml/1fl oz *vegetable oil*

*sea salt and freshly ground black pepper*

*for the marinade*

20g/¾oz *rosemary, leaves picked and finely chopped*

2 *garlic cloves, crushed*

50ml/2fl oz *extra virgin olive oil*

15g/½oz *black peppercorns, crushed*

*for the tomato & olive compote*

6 *plum tomatoes, cut in half lengthwise*

1 *garlic clove, thinly sliced*

200ml/7fl oz *extra virgin olive oil,*

*plus extra for drizzling*

50g/2oz *black olives, pitted and roughly chopped*

10 *basil leaves, torn*

*for the artichoke mash*

300ml/½ pint *extra virgin olive oil*

50g/2oz *spring onions, sliced*

125g/4oz *artichoke purée, bought from a good*

*delicatessen, or see page 156 for homemade version*

50g/2oz *freshly grated Pecorino*

400g/13oz *mashed potato*

20g/¾oz *flat-leaf parsley, finely chopped*

For this recipe the lamb is marinated 24 hours, and the tomatoes cooked 4 hours, in advance.

1  For the marinade, in a bowl mix together the rosemary, garlic, olive oil and peppercorns.

2  Rub the marinade all over the lamb. Season, then cover with plastic wrap or foil and leave to marinate in the refrigerator for 24 hours.

3  To make the tomato & olive compote, preheat oven to 110°C (225°F), Gas Mark ¼. Meanwhile, lay the tomato halves on a baking sheet and place a slice of garlic on top of each.

4  Drizzle with olive oil, season and bake in the oven for 4 hours, then cut into dice.

5  In a bowl, mix the tomatoes with the olives and basil. Stir in the olive oil and season to taste.

6  For the artichoke mash, in a large heavy-based frying pan, heat the olive oil. Add the spring onions and sauté until soft.

7  Next, combine the artichoke purée and Pecorino with the spring onions. Transfer the mashed potatoes to a large bowl and stir in the contents of the frying pan. Add parsley, season to taste and set aside.

8  Preheat oven to 190°C (375°F), Gas Mark 5. To cook the lamb, heat a thick pan until it begins to smoke, about 2 minutes. Add the vegetable oil and colour the lamb, fat side down, then colour all sides golden brown. Transfer to oven and cook for about 8 minutes. Remove from oven and leave in a warm place for 8 minutes before slicing. Slice with the fat at the top into thin even slices.

9  To serve, reheat the artichoke mash in a warm oven for 5–6 minutes and place some in the centre of each plate. Arrange the lamb slices on top with a few spoonfuls of compote. Sprinkle with sea salt and drizzle with olive oil.

• *Serve with Cabernet Sauvignon.*

# liver Veneziana

300g/10oz *onions, thinly sliced from root to shoot*

*pork fat (see below)*

625g/1lb 5oz *calf's liver, skinned, sinew removed and cut into slivers (your butcher can do this for you)*

*salt and freshly ground black pepper*

**for the polenta**

575ml/19fl oz *vegetable stock (see page 20)*

2 *garlic cloves, crushed*

1 *bay leaf*

400g/13oz *white polenta*

*butter for greasing*

50g/2oz *grated Pecorino*

**for the pork fat**

400g/13oz *lardo (solid pork fat), cut into small dice*

100ml/3½fl oz *vegetable oil*

100ml/3½fl oz *water*

25g/1oz *rosemary*

25g/1oz *sage*

25g/1oz *oregano*

25g/1oz *marjoram*

25g/1oz *basil*

**for the garnish**

*extra virgin olive oil for deep-frying*

20 *sage leaves*

1  To make the polenta, preheat the oven to 180°C (350°F), Gas Mark 4. Meanwhile, in a large heavy-based saucepan, heat the vegetable stock and add the garlic and bay leaf.

2  Slowly whisk in the polenta over the heat and gently simmer, stirring occasionally, for 40 minutes. Season well.

3  Grease the inside of 4 ramekins with butter, then line the base and sides with Pecorino, pressing down hard with your fingertips. Add the polenta mixture and press down as before. Bake in the oven for 20 minutes until firm to the touch and set aside.

4  Meanwhile, warm a large, heavy-based saucepan and add the lardo. Next, add the vegetable oil, pour in the water and stir together. Leave to gently simmer for about 4 hours until the fat has dissolved and the water has evaporated.

5  Pass the mixture through a fine sieve into a large bowl and add the herbs while still hot.

6  Leave to cool, then cover and leave the pork fat to set in the refrigerator, about 1 hour.

7  Then warm a large heavy-based frying pan and add a third of the pork fat. Once the fat has melted, remove the herbs, add the onions and slowly cook for about 1 hour, stirring occasionally, until the onions are transparent.

8  When close to serving, preheat oven to 200°C (400°F), Gas Mark 6 and reheat the polenta for 5 minutes. Heat a large, heavy-based frying pan and add the remaining pork fat.

9  Season the liver well and add it to the frying pan. Sauté for 2 minutes, then turn it over. Add the cooked onions and check the seasoning. Sauté for a further 1–2 minutes. Meanwhile, heat some olive oil in a deep-fryer to 200°C (400°F). Deep-fry the sage leaves, about 1–2 minutes, until crispy. Drain on kitchen paper.

10  Turn the polenta out of the ramekins and serve to the side of the liver topped with the onions. Garnish with deep-fried sage leaves.

• *Serve with Merlot.*

# pan-fried foie gras with artichoke röstis, cipolline & balsamic dressing

25g/1oz *butter*

50g/2oz *cipolline (baby onions), finely sliced*

15ml/½fl oz *white wine vinegar*

125g/4oz *rocket, freshly picked (if possible)*

4 x 150g/5oz *foie gras, 2½cm/1in thick*

*8-year-old balsamic vinegar for drizzling*

*salt and freshly ground black pepper*

*for the artichoke röstis*

220g/7¼oz *potatoes, freshly grated*

60g/2½oz *artichoke purée (bought from a good delicatessen or see below for homemade version)*

15g/½oz *rosemary, leaves picked and finely chopped*

100ml/3½fl oz *clarified butter* (see method, page 128)

1  Preheat oven to 190°C (375°F), Gas Mark 5 Meanwhile, warm a large heavy-based frying pan. Melt the butter and sauté the cipolline, shaking the pan occasionally until they are cooked without colouring, about 10 minutes.

2  Add the vinegar to the pan and reduce it away, about 5 minutes. Remove cipolline and reserve.

3  To make the artichoke röstis, wrap the potatoes inside a cloth and squeeze over a draining board. Drain off the excess liquid. In a large bowl, mix the potatoes with the artichoke purée, rosemary and seasoning to taste.

4  Over a high heat on top of the stove, heat a small ovenproof frying pan and add the clarified butter. Pack in a quarter of the potato mixture. Bake in the oven for 10 minutes, then flip the rösti and bake for a further 10 minutes. Remove from pan and keep warm. Repeat 4 times.

5  To serve, place a rösti in the centre of each plate. Reheat the cipolline in a large heavy-based frying pan, about 5 minutes. Add the rocket and toss with the cipolline until it becomes limp. Place this mixture on the röstis.

6  Season the foie gras and quickly warm the frying pan again. Sauté the foie gras for 1 minute on each side and serve it on top of the rocket. Drizzle the juices from the pan around the outside of each plate, then drizzle balsamic vinegar over the juices.

• *Serve with Merlot.*

 *For a homemade version of the artichoke purée, cook 5 globe artichokes, peeled and choke removed, in water with salt and lemon juice for 20 minutes. Then roughly purée in a food processor. If, however, you can find a good readymade purée in your delicatessen you will save yourself the effort of peeling the artichokes.*

# roast guinea fowl with Vin Santo & grapes

125g/4oz *butter, softened at room temperature*

20g/¼oz *rosemary, leaves picked and finely chopped*

20g/¼oz *oregano, leaves picked and finely chopped*

1 *garlic clove, crushed with salt to a purée*

4 x 250g/8oz *guinea fowl, breast and thighs deboned (your butcher can do this for you)*

*extra virgin olive oil for frying*

80g/3¼oz *seedless grapes, peeled*

100ml/3½fl oz *Vin Santo*

200ml/7fl oz *guinea fowl stock (follow chicken stock recipe on page 21 but substitute guinea fowl bones)*

125g/4oz *baby spinach leaves*

20 *baby potatoes, peeled, diced and sautéed in butter with 2 sage leaves for about 15 minutes*

*salt and freshly ground black pepper*

1 Preheat oven to 180°C (350°F), Gas Mark 4. Meanwhile, place the butter in a large bowl and mix in the herbs and garlic. Season well. Lift the skin from the guinea fowl breasts and thighs and rub the butter over them, replacing skin.

2 Warm a large heavy-based ovenproof frying pan, pour in enough oil to cover the base and add the grapes and guinea fowl. Seal the guinea fowl pieces on both sides, about 2 minutes.

3 Transfer the pan to the oven and bake the guinea fowl for 6–7 minutes, turning halfway through (the skin should still be pink). Remove pan from oven. Remove breasts and thighs, cutting each thigh into 3, and keep warm.

4 For the sauce, remove excess fat from the pan and deglaze with Vin Santo over a high heat. Reduce until the alcohol has burnt away. Add the stock and the thigh slices (to increase the flavour) and reduce by half, about 6–7 minutes.

5 Add the baby spinach leaves and toss until limp, then add the pre-cooked potatoes.

6 To serve, place some of the sauce in the centre of each plate. Slice each guinea fowl breast into 4 and arrange on top.

• *Serve with Chianti Classico.*

# braised lamb shank with fava bean mash

100ml/3½fl oz *vegetable oil*

4 *lamb shanks*

125g/4oz *carrots, roughly chopped*

125g/4oz *leeks, outer leaves removed, thoroughly washed and roughly chopped*

125g/4oz *celery, roughly chopped*

125g/4oz *onions, roughly chopped*

½ *garlic bulb, cut in half lengthwise*

1 *rosemary sprig*

8 *plum tomatoes (use the ripest you can find), peeled and roughly chopped*

2 litres/3½ pints *lamb stock (follow veal stock recipe on page 21 but substitute lamb bones for veal)*

50g/2oz *fava (broad) beans, peeled, to garnish*

*salt and freshly ground black pepper*

### for the fava bean mash

50ml/2fl oz *olive oil*

50g/2oz *onions, diced*

1 *garlic clove, crushed with salt into a purée*

25g/1oz *pancetta, roughly chopped*

200g/7oz *fava (broad) beans*

500ml/17fl oz *vegetable stock (see page 20)*

100ml/3½fl oz *double cream*

125g/4oz *butter*

400g/13oz *mashed potato*

50g/2oz *freshly grated Pecorino*

1 Preheat oven to 180°C (350°F), Gas Mark 4. Warm a large flameproof and ovenproof casserole and add the vegetable oil. When the oil is smoking, about 2 minutes, put in the seasoned lamb shanks and seal on all sides until golden brown, about 8–10 minutes, and remove from casserole.

2 Add the carrots, leeks, celery, onions, garlic and rosemary to the casserole. Sauté until the vegetables are golden brown, about 15 minutes, tossing occasionally. Add the tomatoes and continue to cook, stirring occasionally, until the tomatoes break down into a sauce.

3 Stir in the lamb stock and bring to the boil. Add the lamb shanks to the casserole and season. Cover with a lid or foil and bake in the oven for 2–2½ hours until the meat almost falls off the bone. (After 1½ hours remove the lid or foil to allow the meat to brown.)

4 Meanwhile, to make the fava bean mash, warm a large heavy-based saucepan and add the olive oil. When hot, add the onions, garlic and pancetta and sauté for 5 minutes, tossing occasionally.

5 Add the fava beans and vegetable stock to the saucepan. Cook until the fava beans are soft.

6 Pass the beans in liquid through a food mill.

7 In a large heavy-based saucepan, bring the cream and butter to the boil, stirring. Add the mashed potato and stir it in well.

8 Finally, stir in the fava bean purée and the Pecorino. Check the seasoning and set aside.

## chargrilled chicken with porcini

9  When the lamb is cooked, transfer it to a plate and keep warm. Reheat the mash in the pan, about 2 minutes. Meanwhile, pass the cooking liquid from the lamb through a fine sieve. Reduce down to the desired consistency in a small pan and check the seasoning.

10 Reheat the sauce and add the peeled fava beans. Cook the beans in the sauce for 1–2 minutes, stirring occasionally. Season. To serve, place some mash in the centre of each plate, top with a lamb shank and pour over the sauce.

• *Serve with Cabernet del Trentino.*

---

4 x 200g/7oz *chicken supreme, boned, skinned and sinews removed (your butcher can do this for you)*

200ml/7fl oz *garlic oil (see page 10), plus extra for brushing*

400g/13oz *fresh porcini, cut into 3mm/⅛in slices*

20g/¾oz *flat-leaf parsley (freshly picked, if possible), coarsely chopped*

*truffle oil for drizzling*

*salt and freshly ground black pepper*

---

1  Cut the chicken pieces almost in half horizontally (do not cut completely through) so that they open out flat like a book.

2  Place a piece of plastic wrap underneath each chicken piece, and another one on top. Use a meat hammer to beat the chicken until it measures about 18–20cm/7–8in in diameter. Remove the plastic wrap.

3  Brush each chicken breast with garlic oil and season well. Place on a preheated chargrill, or under a grill, and cook for 3 minutes each side.

4  Meanwhile, heat the garlic oil in a large heavy-based frying pan. When hot, add the porcini. Cook until golden brown, about 3 minutes, then repeat on the other side. Season well and add the parsley.

5  To serve, place a chicken breast in the centre of each plate. Tip some of the porcini over the top of each chicken piece and scatter the remainder around the plates. Finally, add a drizzle of truffle oil.

• *Serve with Chardonnay.*

# herb-crusted rack of lamb with courgettes, fava beans, pancetta & mint

2 racks of lamb (8 bones each)

vegetable oil for frying

2 tsps Dijon mustard

50g/2oz pancetta strips

2 artichokes, cut into wedges

125g/4oz courgettes, cut into cubes and sautéed in a little extra virgin olive oil

50g/2oz fava (broad) beans, peeled, blanched in boiling salted water for 1 minute, then plunged into cold water

4 mint leaves

200ml/7fl oz veal stock (see page 21), boiled to reduce by half

salt and freshly ground black pepper

**for the herb crust**

200g/7oz ciabatta, roughly torn into pieces

40g/2½oz lemon rind, roughly cut into strips

40g/2½oz capers, rinsed

40g/2½oz anchovies, tinned or fresh

40g/2½oz onions, roughly chopped

40g/2½oz black olives, pitted and roughly chopped

1 bunch each parsley and basil

For this recipe the herb crust needs to be prepared at least 2 hours in advance.

 *Remember to allow the lamb to rest for 5–10 minutes after cooking. This allows the juices to settle and disperse through the meat, keeping it tender.*

1  First, make the herb crust. Preheat oven to 120°C (250°F), Gas Mark ½ and lay the ciabatta, lemon rind, capers, anchovies, onions and olives on a baking sheet. Place them in the oven to dry out for 2 hours.

2  Transfer the mixture to the bowl of a food processor fitted with the metal blade and whiz until fine breadcrumbs form, about 2 minutes.

3  Add the herbs and whiz until the mixture becomes a bright-green colour, about 2 minutes.

4  Preheat oven to 180°C (350°F), Gas Mark 4. Season the lamb and then warm a large heavy-based frying pan. Add enough oil to cover the base and seal the meat on the side with fat, about 2 minutes.

5  Brush the lamb with mustard so that it is completely covered and then roll it in the herb crust. Place the meat in a shallow baking dish and bake in the oven until medium rare, about 12 minutes, turning halfway through. Remove from the oven and leave to rest.

6  While the lamb is cooking, warm a frying pan and add the pancetta and then the artichoke wedges. Season well.

7  Stir in the courgettes, fava beans and mint leaves and add a little warmed veal stock to bring the mixture together. Keep warm.

8  To serve, cut the lamb racks into cutlets. On each plate arrange a few cutlets on a bed of vegetable mixture. Drizzle veal stock around the outside of each plate.

• *Serve with Bordeaux.*

# beef tagliata with tomato, aubergine & basil compote

*tomato, aubergine & basil compote* (see page 16)

*4 x 160g/5½oz fillet steaks*

*sea salt and freshly ground black pepper*

1  Prepare the tomato, aubergine & basil compote, or, if already made and stored in refrigerator, remove and bring to room temperature, or heat gently in a pan, as preferred.

2  On a very hot griddle pan or grill plate, sear the steaks on both sides for 4–5 minutes (for medium-rare) and allow to rest for 5 minutes.

3  To serve, place the aubergine and tomato mixture in the centre of each plate. Slice the beef thinly and arrange on top. Drizzle juices from the frying pan around the plate and season with sea salt.

• *Serve with Sangiovese.*

# costaletta Milanese

4 x 175–250g/8–9oz *veal cutlets, tenderised with a meat hammer and cut into thin slices no more than 8-10mm/¼in thick*

200g/7oz *rocket, roughly chopped*

6 *plum tomatoes, finely diced*

25ml/1fl oz *extra virgin olive oil*

100ml/3½fl oz *clarified butter (see method, page 128)*

100ml/3½fl oz *vegetable oil*

4 *lemon wedges, to garnish*

*salt and freshly ground black pepper*

*for the coating*

1 *egg, beaten*

100ml/3½fl oz *milk*

pinch *freshly grated nutmeg*

200g/7oz *fresh breadcrumbs*

50g/2oz *freshly grated Parmesan*

This dish is traditionally served with a bowl of tomato and basil spaghetti (see page 146).

1 For the coating, mix the egg, milk and nutmeg in a bowl. Mix the breadcrumbs and Parmesan in a bowl. Season the veal slices, immerse in the milk and then the breadcrumb mixtures.

2 In a large bowl, mix together the rocket and tomatoes with a little olive oil.

3 In a heavy-based frying pan, heat the clarified butter and vegetable oil together until almost smoking, about 6 minutes. Add the veal slices and sauté, shaking the frying pan continually until golden, about 2–3 minutes each side.

4 To serve, put some salad in the centre of each plate. Place the veal on top and garnish with a lemon wedge. Season well.

• *Serve with Chianti.*

# seared foie gras with endive, pear & Vin Santo

4 x 150g/5oz *foie gras slices*

*extra virgin olive oil for frying*

2 *endives, roots removed and cut into quarters*

1 *pear, peeled, cored and cut into slices*

100ml/3½fl oz *Vin Santo*

50g/2oz *pine nuts, toasted (see page 13)*

50g/2oz *baby spinach leaves*

8-year-old balsamic vinegar for drizzling

*salt and freshly ground black pepper*

1 Season the foie gras and warm a large heavy-based frying pan. Add enough olive oil to cover the base of the pan and sauté the foie gras for 1 minute on each side. Remove and keep warm.

2 Add the endives to the pan. Sauté for 1 minute, then add the pear slices and sauté for a further 3 minutes, tossing the mixture occasionally to prevent it sticking.

3 Next, add the Vin Santo to the pan and reduce the mixture by two-thirds. Add the pine nuts and baby spinach leaves. Toss the contents of the pan together and check the seasoning.

4 To serve, place some of the vegetable mixture in the centre of each plate and sit the foie gras on top. To finish, drizzle balsamic vinegar around the outside of each plate.

• *Serve with Barbaresco.*

# desserts

blood orange & polenta cake
with mascarpone ice cream

crème brûlée

tiramisu

Amaretti ice cream

pistachio ice cream

Cantuccini ice cream

mascarpone ice cream

chocolate ice cream

pistachio tuiles

apple crostata with Amaretti ice cream

peach zabaglione

chocolate & polenta cake

pear & fig tart

pots au chocolat

white peach & Prosecco panna cotta

 AFTER A MEAL WHICH MIGHT INCLUDE ANTIPASTI AND PASTA OR RISOTTO, THEN MEAT OR FISH, DESSERT NEEDS TO BE LIGHT AND REFRESHING, LIKE ICE CREAM AND FRESH FRUIT, CREAMY TIRAMISU OR ONE OF THE MANY KINDS OF TORTA DELLA NONNA (GRANDMOTHER'S CAKE) MADE WITH ALMONDS.

**figs** Figs have an integral place in Italian food, whether served after a meal or to start, with a plate of prosciutto. Look for plump, juicy, ripe ones that feel soft to the touch, as if they were almost ready to burst. Hard, unripe figs are a huge disappointment.

**pears** Pears match well with cheese, such as Gorgonzola and Pecorino, which are often mixed together in salads. As with figs and peaches it is safest to buy pears when they are in season, when you have the pick of the sweet, juicy, ripe fruit.

**peaches** There is something very sensual about the fresh, downy, fleshy peach. The best are straight from the tree, bursting with juice and sweetness, so when buying them look for ones that come closest in flavour and sensation. To many tastes the aromatic white-fleshed peaches are the finest, and these are certainly the ones to use for Bellinis, the great Italian summer drink made with white peach purée and sparkling Prosecco wine or champagne. White peaches also make a fine compote for serving with Prosecco and panna cotta (see page 187).

**dates** Fresh dates can be either soft and moist or hard and quite fibrous, but in Europe the dates most people recognise are semi-dried. They are very high in sugar content, and at Daphne's are used mainly in the making of dessert biscuits.

# lemons
Some of the best-quality lemons to be found are Sicilian, still on the branch: big, irregular, with bumps and marks and a colour ranging through green and yellow. They are a world apart from the uniform lemons in shiny waxed jackets sold in most supermarkets. They have thick skins and pith, which are good for zest, and an intensely natural flavour of fruit. Otherwise look for organic, unwaxed lemons. When buying lemons specifically for their juice, in general the thinner the skin the more juice in the fruit.

# mascarpone
Used extensively in desserts, this thick creamy cheese made from cow's milk can do the work of double cream, but without the heaviness and cloying texture. Its most famous use is in tiramisu, but it also makes an excellent quick and foolproof custard for serving with a fruit tart. The mascarpone simply needs to be brought to the boil with a vanilla pod, split lengthways and the seeds scraped out, a little caster sugar and a dash or two of Amaretti liqueur, then it can be taken straight off the heat and it is ready. Because the custard contains no eggs, it won't separate or curdle.

# vanilla
Handle vanilla pods carefully and they will last a long time. The real vanilla intensity is concentrated around the seeds, but even when these have been scraped out to flavour crème brûlée or ice cream, or a pan of red wine being used to poach pears, the pods still retain a great deal of flavour. They can be rinsed, dried and then stored in a jar of caster sugar to make vanilla sugar, which can then be used in desserts.

# ice creams and sorbets
Hazelnut, chocolate, pistachio and walnut ice cream are all favourites at Daphne's along with vanilla ice cream, flavoured with crushed Amaretto or Cantuccini biscuits, and vibrant sorbets, such as blood orange. Vanilla ice cream is all about the quality of the custard; while with sorbets the important point is the relationship between sugar, water and acidity. Ice creams and sorbets are something that you need to feel your way with; the more you make them, the more you will begin to instinctively understand if they are working to your liking. Homemade ice creams and sorbets should be made in small quantities and consumed as soon as possible.

# farmhouse cheeses
In general Italian cheeses tend to be rather creamier and milder than their more assertive French counterparts. At Daphne's a cheese plate might consist of three cow's-milk cheeses: the soft, creamy blue-veined Dolcelatte; Gorgonzola, stronger in flavour, also streaked with blue; and Taleggio, with its orange rind, a kind of cross between Brie and Port-Salut. There may also be some Pecorino and Parmesan, all served with thin wafers in the style of the famous Sardinian 'music' bread, walnut bread or Cantuccini-style biscuits made with hazelnuts and raisins.

# crème brûlée

250ml/8fl oz *double cream*

2 *vanilla pods*

2 *eggs*

60g/2½oz *caster sugar*

*demerara sugar for sprinkling*

1 Preheat oven to 110°C (225°F), Gas Mark ¼. Meanwhile, pour the cream into a large heavy-based saucepan. Split the vanilla pods, scrape out the seeds and add both seeds and pods to the cream. Slowly bring the mixture to boiling point, stirring, and remove the saucepan from the heat immediately.

2 Whisk the eggs and caster sugar in a bowl over a pan of boiling water until thickened. Remove from the heat and whisk in the cream. Remove pods from the cream.

3 Transfer the mixture to four ramekins and place them on top of a baking tray. Bake in the oven for 25–35 minutes until just undercooked. (The mixture should move just slightly when the side is tapped with a spoon.) Remove the ramekins from the oven and leave to cool, then refrigerate, covered, until needed.

4 To serve, heat the grill and sprinkle demerara sugar over the top of each ramekin. Place the ramekins under the grill for 1 minute or until the sugar has caramelised. Serve immediately.

• *Serve with Moscato D'Asti dessert wine.*

# blood orange & polenta cake with mascarpone ice cream

325g/11oz *butter, plus extra for greasing*

325g/11oz *caster sugar*

325g/11oz *ground almonds*

5g/¼oz *baking powder*

4 *eggs, beaten*

160g/5½oz *fine yellow polenta*

4 *blood oranges, juice squeezed and rind cut into thin strips*

*mascarpone ice cream* (see page 178), *to serve*

1 Preheat oven to 160°C (325°F), Gas Mark 3. Butter a 30cm/12in spring-release tin and line the base with non-stick baking paper.

2 In a large bowl, cream together the butter and sugar until pale, about 8 minutes.

3 Fold in the almonds and then the baking powder. Beat in the eggs, one by one, and stir in the polenta, orange juice and rind.

4 Scrape the mixture into the prepared tin and bake in the centre of the oven for 30 minutes until firm. Test with a skewer to check.

5 To serve, divide the cake into wedges and serve with scoops of mascarpone ice cream.

• *Serve with Trocolato dessert wine.*

# tiramisu

2 eggs, separated

75g/3oz caster sugar

60ml/2¼fl oz Marsala

25ml/1fl oz Kahlua

500g/1lb mascarpone cheese

500g/1lb sponge cake, cut into fingers

sifted cocoa powder for dusting

**for soaking the sponge**

250ml/8fl oz espresso coffee

50ml/2fl oz Kahlua

125g/4oz caster sugar

This dish needs to be started at least 3–4 hours before serving.

1 In a bowl over a bain-marie (or pan of water) placed over low heat, whisk the 2 egg yolks, 1 egg white and the caster sugar together until slightly thick, about 3 minutes. Still whisking, remove the bowl from the heat and continue until the mixture becomes cold. (This mixture is known as a sabayon.)

2 Warm the Marsala and Kahlua together in a saucepan. Pour the alcohol into the egg and sugar mixture and whisk together thoroughly.

3 Beat the mascarpone cheese into the mixture until it binds completely and becomes smooth and thick, about 3 minutes. Set aside.

4 In a bowl, place the coffee, Kahlua and sugar. Dip the sponge cake into the mixture to soak it quickly, then cover the base of a serving dish with soaked sponge strips.

5 Add a layer of the mascarpone mixture then another layer of sponge. Continue placing alternate layers to fill the dish, ending with a layer of mascarpone. Cover and refrigerate until set, preferably 12 hours but at least 2.

6 Just before serving, dust some cocoa powder lightly over the surface and serve immediately.

• *Serve with Avie Moscato, Moscato D'Asti, or other dessert wine that is not overly sweet.*

# Amaretti ice cream

3 egg yolks

75g/3oz caster sugar

150ml/¼ pint milk

150ml/¼ pint double cream

1 vanilla pod

125g/4oz Amaretti biscuits, crushed

100ml/3½fl oz Amaretto liqueur

1  In a large heatproof bowl, slowly whisk together the egg yolks and caster sugar until light in colour, about 10 minutes.

2  In a large heavy-based saucepan, combine the milk and cream. Scrape the vanilla seeds out of the pod into the saucepan, using a knife, then add the pod. Slowly bring the mixture to just below boiling point.

3  Pour a little warm cream into the egg yolks and combine. Continue adding cream until the two mixtures are completely combined.

4  Transfer the mixture to a clean saucepan and cook it gently over a low heat, stirring constantly to prevent it curdling. When thickened and almost at boiling point, pour the mixture into a bowl and leave to cool. Discard the vanilla pod.

5  Fold the Amaretti biscuits and the Amaretto liqueur into the cooled mixture.

6  Pour the mixture into an ice-cream machine and churn until frozen according to manufacturer's directions, or freeze in a suitable container.

7  To serve, transfer the ice cream to the refrigerator 15 minutes before serving so that it is nice and soft. Serve in scoops.

• *Serve with Vin Santo dessert wine.*

# pistachio ice cream

3 egg yolks

75g/3oz caster sugar

150ml/¼ pint milk

150ml/¼ pint double cream

50g/2oz pistachio paste

(available from any good delicatessen)

125g/4oz shelled pistachio nuts, crushed

1  Follow step 1 for making Amaretti ice cream (see left).

2  In a large heavy-based saucepan, combine the milk and cream. Slowly bring the mixture to just below boiling point.

3  Follow step 3 for making Amaretti ice cream.

4  Transfer the mixture to a clean saucepan and cook gently over a low heat, stirring constantly to prevent it curdling. When thickened and almost at boiling point, pour the mixture into a bowl.

5  Whisk in the pistachio paste and leave to cool. Fold in the pistachio nuts.

6  Follow steps 6 and 7 for making Amaretti ice cream.

• *Serve with Vin Santo dessert wine.*

CHOCOLATE, AMARETTI AND PISTACHIO ICE
CREAM IN A PISTACHIO TUILE.

# Cantuccini ice cream

| |
|---|
| 3 *egg yolks* |
| 75g/3oz *caster sugar* |
| 150ml/¼ pint *milk* |
| 150ml/¼ pint *double cream* |
| 1 *vanilla pod* |
| 125g/4oz *Cantuccini biscuits, crushed* |

1 Follow steps 1, 2, 3 and 4 for making Amaretti ice cream (see page 176).
2 Fold in the Cantuccini biscuits.
3 Follow steps 6 and 7 for making Amaretti ice cream.

• *Serve with Vin Santo dessert wine.*

# mascarpone ice cream

| |
|---|
| 3 *egg yolks* |
| 75g/3oz *caster sugar* |
| 150ml/¼ pint *milk* |
| 150ml/¼ pint *double cream* |
| 125g/4oz *mascarpone* |

1 Follow step 1 for making Amaretti ice cream (see page 176).
2 In a large heavy-based saucepan, combine the milk and cream. Slowly bring the mixture to just below boiling point.
3 Follow step 3 for making Amaretti ice cream.
4 Transfer the mixture to a clean saucepan and cook gently over low heat, stirring constantly to prevent it curdling. When thickened and almost at boiling point, pour the mixture into a bowl and leave to cool.
5 Fold in the mascarpone.
6 Follow steps 6 and 7 for making Amaretti ice cream.

• *Serve with Vin Santo dessert wine.*

# chocolate ice cream

3 *egg yolks*

75g/3oz *caster sugar*

150ml/¼ pint *milk*

150ml/¼ pint *double cream*

60g/2½oz *dark couverture chocolate (53–57% cocoa content), shaved*

1 Follow step 1 for making Amaretti ice cream (see page 176), then combine the milk and cream in a large heavy-based saucepan. Slowly bring the mixture to just below boiling point.

2 Follow step 3 for making Amaretti ice cream.

3 Transfer the mixture to a clean saucepan and cook it gently over a low heat, stirring constantly to prevent it curdling. When thickened and almost at boiling point, pour the mixture into a bowl.

4 Add the chocolate and continue stirring until it has dissolved. Leave the mixture to cool.

5 Follow steps 6 and 7 for Amaretti ice cream.

• *Serve with Vin Santo dessert wine.*

# pistachio tuiles

100g/3½oz *butter*

125g/4oz *icing sugar*

3 *egg whites*

100g/3½oz *plain flour*

25g/1oz *shelled pistachio nuts, roughly chopped*

1 In a large bowl, cream the butter and icing sugar together until the mixture becomes white, about 8 minutes.

2 Fold in the egg whites and slowly fold in the flour, working the mixture in a figure-of-eight. Transfer to a plastic container and leave, covered, to rest for 2 hours.

3 Preheat oven to 180°C (350°F), Gas Mark 4. Meanwhile, lay a sheet of non-stick baking paper out on a baking tray and spread the creamed mixture out thinly on the surface to make 4 circles. Sprinkle pistachio nuts around the edge of each circle.

4 Bake in the centre of the oven for 4-5 minutes until golden brown. When cooked, remove immediately from tray and shape each over an upturned dariole mould, or deep upturned bowl. Leave to cool.

 *Serve the pistachio tuiles filled with Amaretti, chocolate, Cantuccini, pistachio or mascarpone ice creams, as pictured on page 177.*

# apple crostata with Amaretti ice cream

| |
|---|
| *plain flour for rolling out* |
| 1kg/2lb *puff pastry* |
| 4 *Granny Smith apples, peeled, cored* |
| *and cut in half lengthwise* |
| 1 tbsp *caster sugar* |
| 1 tsp *ground cinnamon* |
| *butter for greasing* |
| 4 scoops *Amaretti ice cream* (see page 176) |
| 1 tsp *sifted cocoa powder, to serve* |

**for the apricot glaze**

| |
|---|
| 2 tbsps *apricot jam* |
| 2 tbsps *water* |

1  Preheat oven to 180°C (350°F), Gas Mark 4. Meanwhile, on a floured surface, roll the pastry out to 3mm/⅛in thick. Use a 15cm/6in pastry cutter to cut out 4 rounds. Then use a 5cm/2in cutter to cut out a hole in the centre of each one to form rings.

2  Slice the apples into thin semicircles. Lay the slices around the inner edge of each pastry ring, leaving a 3mm/⅛in border. Use a cocktail stick to flute the outer edges.

3  In a small bowl, mix together the caster sugar and cinnamon. Sprinkle the mixture over the apples.

4  Place the pastries on a greased baking sheet and bake in the oven for 15–20 minutes until risen and golden brown.

# peach zabaglione

| |
|---|
| 3 *ripe peaches, peeled, halved and stones removed* |
| 50ml/2fl oz *Marsala* |
| 10 *egg yolks* |
| 175g/6oz *caster sugar* |
| 125ml/4fl oz *double cream, lightly whipped* |
| *icing sugar for dusting* |

5  Meanwhile, make the apricot glaze. In a small saucepan over low heat, dissolve the jam with the water, stirring continuously. Keep warm.

6  Remove the pastries from the oven and brush with the apricot glaze. Transfer to dessert plates.

7  To serve, place a scoopful of Amaretti ice cream in the centre of each pastry and sprinkle with cocoa powder.

• *Serve with Vin Santo dessert wine.*

The peaches need to be prepared 2–3 hours before serving time. Parfait glasses should be chilled half an hour before serving time.

1  Dice 4 peach halves into 5mm/¼in pieces, reserving the other 2 halves for serving.

2  Heat a large heavy-based frying pan. Add the peaches and Marsala and cook over a high heat until the alcohol has burnt out and most of the liquid has been absorbed, about 8 minutes. Remove from heat, leave to cool, then refrigerate, covered, for 2 hours until chilled.

3  When the peaches have chilled, whisk the egg yolks and sugar together in a large bowl until thick, about 10 minutes. Gently fold in the whipped cream and peaches.

4  Divide the mixture among 4 chilled parfait glasses. Cut the remaining 2 peach halves in half and thinly slice almost to the bottom. Gently fan out and place a fan on top of each dessert. To finish, dust with icing sugar.

• *Serve with Marsala dessert wine.*

*When whisking egg yolks and sugar together to make a sabayon (as above), never do so in an aluminium bowl as its acidity will react with the sabayon and discolour it. Always use a glass, ceramic, stainless steel or copper bowl for this process.*

# chocolate & polenta cake

| |
|---|
| 325g/11oz *butter, plus extra for greasing* |
| *plain flour for dusting* |
| 325g/11oz *caster sugar* |
| 300g/10oz *ground almonds* |
| 35g/1½oz *cocoa powder, sifted* |
| 4 *eggs, beaten* |
| 160g/5½oz *fine yellow polenta* |
| 5g/¼oz *baking powder* |
| 1 tsp *almond essence* |

1  Preheat oven to 160°C (325°F), Gas Mark 3. Line a 30cm/12in cake tin with baking paper, then grease and flour it.
2  In a large bowl, cream together the butter and sugar until pale, about 8 minutes.
3  Stir in the almonds and cocoa powder. Beat in the eggs, one at a time, and fold in the remaining ingredients.
4  Spoon into the prepared tin. Bake in the centre of the oven for 30 minutes or until golden brown with the surface starting to crack.
5  Serve warm with the ice cream of your choice.

• *Serve with Avie Moscato dessert wine.*

# pear & fig tart

**for the sweetpaste**

125g/4oz *unsalted butter, plus extra for greasing*

125g/4oz *icing sugar, sifted*

1 *egg, beaten*

1 *egg yolk*

250g/8oz *plain flour, sifted*

**for the filling**

6 *pears, peeled, cored and sliced*

3 *figs, cut into eighths*

200g/7oz *caster sugar*

125g/4oz *butter*

juice of 1 *lemon*

½ tsp *mixed spice*

**for the crumble**

150g/5oz *unsalted butter*

150g/5oz *plain flour, sifted*

150g/5oz *caster sugar*

75g/3oz *ground almonds*

75g/3oz *chopped mixed nuts*

The sweetpaste for this recipe needs to be prepared 2 hours in advance.

1  In a large bowl, whisk together the butter and icing sugar until white, about 8 minutes. Gradually whisk in the egg and egg yolk. Fold in the flour, working the mixture as little as possible. Refrigerate, covered, for 2 hours.

2  Preheat oven to 180°C (350°F), Gas Mark 4. Meanwhile, line a greased 30cm/12in flan ring with the sweetpaste and bake blind for 10 minutes until firm. Leave to cool on a cooling rack. Keep the oven on.

3  Place the ingredients for the filling in a heavy-based saucepan. Bring to the boil, stirring continuously, then simmer for about 10 minutes or until caramelised. Leave to cool, stirring occasionally.

4  To make the crumble, in a large bowl rub together the butter, flour and sugar until the texture resembles breadcrumbs. Add the nuts and mix together lightly.

5  With a spatula, scrape the filling into the prepared case and top with crumble. Bake in the centre of the oven for about 35 minutes until golden brown.

•  *Serve with Muffato dessert wine.*

# pots au chocolat

250ml/8fl oz *double cream*

75ml/3fl oz *milk*

220g/7¼oz *good-quality dark chocolate*

**for the cenci biscuits**

25g/1oz *butter, softened at room temperature*

50g/2oz *caster sugar*

250g/8oz *flour*

rind of 1 *orange, cut into thin strips*

rind of 1 *lemon, cut into thin strips*

2 *eggs, beaten*

dash of *Marsala*

*vegetable oil for frying*

*sifted icing sugar for dusting*

The pots au chocolat need to be made
4–5 hours in advance.

1 In a large heavy-based saucepan, warm the
cream and milk together. Meanwhile, melt
the dark chocolate, either over a bain-marie
(or pan of boiling water), about 10 minutes,
or in a microwave on low heat.

2 Transfer the melted chocolate to the cream
and milk mixture and mix together thoroughly.

3 Divide the mixture among 4 ramekins or pots.
Leave to cool, then refrigerate, uncovered, until
set, about 4 hours.

4 To make the cenci biscuits, in a bowl cream
together the butter with the caster sugar, then
fold in the flour.

5 Add the citrus rinds, eggs and Marsala to
bind the mixture together and form a firm
dough. Leave, covered, in the refrigerator for
20 minutes.

6 Dust a work surface with icing sugar, then use
a pasta machine or rolling pin to roll the dough
out to a thickness of about 5mm/¼in. Divide it
into large squares.

7 In a large heavy-based frying pan, shallow-fry
the squares in vegetable oil over a medium heat
until golden, about 2 minutes. Drain on kitchen
paper and coat in icing sugar while warm.

8 Place an individual pot au chocolat on each
serving plate accompanied by a few cenci
biscuits. (If preferred, the pots can also be
served with readymade Cantuccini biscuits.)

• *Serve with Trocolato dessert wine.*

# white peach & Prosecco panna cotta

100ml/3½fl oz *milk*

2 *vanilla pods*

400ml/14fl oz *double cream*

5 *egg yolks*

60g/2¼oz *caster sugar*

4 tbsps *Prosecco or other sparkling wine*

7 *mint leaves, finely chopped, to serve*

*for the peach compote*

150ml/¼ pint *water*

60g/2½oz *granulated sugar*

½ *lemon*

½ *lime*

1 *vanilla pod*

2 *white peaches, skinned, pitted and diced*

The panna cotta needs to be made at least 4–5 hours, and the peach compote 2 hours, before serving time.

1   To make the compote, pour the water into a large heavy-based saucepan. Add the sugar, lemon and lime halves. Split the vanilla pod, scrape out the seeds and add both seeds and empty pod. Cook slowly over low heat for 1 hour, stirring occasionally, until a thick syrup has formed.

2   Strain the syrup through a fine sieve into a bowl, then return it to the saucepan. Bring to the boil, then add the peaches.

3   Remove the saucepan from the heat. Remove the empty pod from the syrup, but leave the seeds in. Set aside to cool.

4   To make the panna cotta, place the milk in a large heavy-based saucepan with the vanilla pods, split into seeds and empty pods. Bring the milk to the boil. Remove from heat, stir in the cream and leave to cool.

5   Whisk in the egg yolks and sugar until the cream becomes stiff, about 6 minutes, then stir in the Prosecco. Remove the empty pods.

6   Preheat oven to 120°C (250°F), Gas Mark ½. Meanwhile, divide the mixture among 4 ramekins. Place them in a deep roasting tin and fill the tin with hot water reaching halfway up the ramekins.

7   Bake the panna cotta for about 30–40 minutes until set. Leave to cool, then cover and refrigerate for about 3 hours until set.

8   To serve, turn individual moulds out onto the centre of each plate and spoon peach compote around the outside of the plates. Finally, sprinkle with mint.

• *Serve with Moscato D'Asti dessert wine.*

# SOURCING GUIDE

FOLLOWING ARE SOME SUGGESTIONS FOR FINDING FANTASTICALLY FRESH PRODUCE AND STORE-CUPBOARD STAPLES, BOTH AT SOURCE AND IN KEY CITIES.

## AT SOURCE

### Anchovies

Italy's finest anchovies come from Sicily. For one of the best selections, go to Palermo, the capital, and shop for big fleshy anchovies, along with an excellent variety of other Sicilian specialities such as capers and olives, at:

- Fratelli Raspante
*Corso Pisani 326*
*Palermo (Sicily)*

### Buffalo Mozzarella and Buffalo Ricotta

In and around Naples, fresh buffalo mozzarella and ricotta are made daily from buffalo milk from the farms in the surrounding countryside. The village of Mondragone, a half-hour's drive from Naples in the province of Caserta, is dotted with traditional makers, such as Mandara, making delicious buffalo mozzarella and ricotta.

### Focaccia

The little bakeries in Santa Margherita and Portofino on the Italian Riviera bake great focaccia — very salty, greased in oil and ultra soft — originally made for Genoa's dock workers, who needed to replenish the salt lost as they sweated over their labours.

### Fresh Produce

The Rialto Market, Venice, the world-famous food market by the Grand Canal, is the place to find the finest fresh vegetables: porcini, courgettes with their yellow flowers, asparagus, artichokes, aubergines, radicchio. In the fish market the profusion of fish includes sea bass and monkfish and glorious seafood such as soft-shell crabs, scampi, scallops and clams.

### Olive Oil

Lucca in Tuscany is the traditional centre for olive oil production. Here you will find big-name blenders and makers of commercial olive oils, as well as small estates producing limited quantities of delicious olive oil with the characteristic pepperiness associated with Tuscany. In the streets radiating from the main square of Lucca, delicatessens sell such oils, as do individual estates in the vicinity and elsewhere in Tuscany:

- Frantoio Sanminiatese
*Via Maremmana, 8*
*Località La Serra (Pisa)*

- Fattoria Colleverde Matraia
*Località Matraia (Lucca)*

- Fattoria di Forci
*Località Forci (Lucca)*

- Fattoria di San Vito in Fior di Selva
*Via San Vito, 32*
*Montelupo Fiorentino (Florence)*

### Lentils

An excellent source of Umbria's famed lentils is the small mountain town of Norcia, which is dotted with shops selling the local Lenticchie di Castelluccio, grown on the nearby plains of Castelluccio and considered the best in Italy. Other specialities include farro, black truffles and succulent hams and salumi.

**Pecorino Cheese**

Pecorino cheese is made throughout central
and southern Italy. Tuscany specialises in a tangy
Pecorino cheese known as Pecorino toscano.
Choice stockists and makers include:

- Caseificio Cugusi
  *Via di Gracciano nel Corso, 31*
  *Montepulciano (Siena)*

- Agricola La Parrina
  *Via Aurelia at km 146*
  *Orbetello (Grosseto)*

**Speck**

A speciality of the craggy Dolomite mountain
range bordering Austria, speck is still traditionally
produced by individual farms and small cooperatives,
particularly in the northern part of the Dolomites
called Val Pusteria. An excellent selection of
artisanally made speck can be found at:

- Senfter
  *Via Mercato, 1, San Candido*
  *Val Pusteria*

- Anton Nocker
  *Via Dolomiti, 19-A, Dobbiaco*
  *Val Pusteria*

**White Truffles**

The best white truffles come from Alba. In October
a month-long truffle fair attracts people from all
over the world to this northern Italian town, when
restaurants serve dishes showered with truffle
shavings. A truffle market is held in the town each
Saturday from mid-September to late December.

## FINE FOOD STOCKISTS

**In Italy:**
- Peck
  *Via Spadari, 9*
  *Milan*

- Cantinetta de Verrazzano
  *Via dei Tavolini, 18/20*
  *Florence*

- De Carolis
  *Via Sabotino, 28*
  *Rome*

**In London:**
- Luigi's
  *349 Fulham Road*
  *London SW10 9TW*

- La Fromagerie
  *30 Highbury Park*
  *London N5 2AA*

- Carluccio's
  *28A Neal Street*
  *London WC2H 9PS*

**In New York City:**
- Dean & DeLuca
  *560 Broadway*
  *at Prince Street*

- Balducci's
  *424 Sixth Avenue*
  *at 9th Street*

# INDEX

## ACKNOWLEDGMENTS

The publishers would like to thank the team at Daphne's for their patience and support, in particular Mogens Tholstrup, Chris Benians, Lee Purcell, Steve Mills, Teresa Ivens, Rachel Lyle, Rosario Mauro and Matt Hay.

Kind thanks also to Joanna Bowlby, Jean Cazals, Jane Donovan, Lesley Levine, Martin Lovelock, Danny Michelson at La Fromagerie, and Salvatore Arricale at Mandara UK.